A Psychology of Food

A Psychology of Food

More Than a Matter of Taste

Bernard Lyman, Ph.D.

An **avi** Book
Published by Van Nostrand Reinhold Company
New York

An AVI Book
(AVI is an imprint of Van Nostrand Reinhold Company Inc.)

Copyright © 1989 by Van Nostrand Reinhold Company Inc.
Library of Congress Catalog Card Number 88-5676
ISBN 0-442-25939-5

Printed in the United States of America
Designed by Rosa Delia Vasquez

Van Nostrand Reinhold Company Inc.
115 Fifth Avenue
New York, New York 10003

Van Nostrand Reinhold Company Limited
Molly Millars Lane
Wokingham, Berkshire RG11 2PY, England

Van Nostrand Reinhold
480 La Trobe Street
Melbourne, Victoria 3000, Australia

Macmillan of Canada
Division of Canada Publishing Corporation
164 Commander Boulevard
Agincourt, Ontario M1S 3C7, Canada

16 15 14 13 12 11 10 9 8 7 6 5 4 3 2 1

Library of Congress Cataloging-in-Publication Data
Lyman, Bernard, 1924–
    A psychology of food: more than a matter of taste/Bernard
Lyman.
       p. cm.
    "An AVI book."
    Bibliography: p.
    Includes index.
    ISBN 0-442-25939-5
    1. Food—Psychological aspects. I. Title.
TX357.L94 1989
152.1'6—dc19   88-5676
                                                          CIP

To my sons, Tim, Burt, and Ethan,
with affection and respect

CONTENTS

Contents

PART 4
Food Meanings and Associations

PREFACE

Writing this book has been a pleasure, but it has also been frustrating. It was a delight to see that the facts of food preferences, eating, and food behavior conform in many ways to the general principles of psychology. Matching these, however, was often like putting together a jigsaw puzzle—looking at a fact and trying to figure out which psychological theories or principles were relevant. This was made more difficult by conflicting principles in psychology and contradictory findings in psychological as well as food-preference research.

The material cited is not meant to be exhaustive. Undoubtedly, I have been influenced by my own research interests and points of view. When conflicting data exist, I selected those that seemed to me most representative or relevant, and I have done so without consistently pointing out contrary findings. This applies also to the discussion of psychological principles.

Much psychological research is done in very restrictive conditions. Therefore, it has limited applicability beyond the confines of the context in which it was conducted. What holds true of novelty, complexity, and curiosity when two-dimensional line drawings are studied, for example, may not have much to do with novelty, complexity, and curiosity in relation to foods, which vary in many ways such as shape, color, taste, texture, and odor. Nevertheless, I have tried to suggest relationships between psychological principles and food preferences.

The book is divided into four parts. Part 1 examines the psychological meaning and significance of food, and its role in personality and social development. Part 2 discusses stable and fluctuating food preferences, including the role played by emotions. In Part 3, food is treated as a complex stimulus based on its sensory qualities of taste, odor, texture, appearance, and color. Reference to associations and food meanings is made throughout the book, but they are the primary focus in Part 4, which deals also with preferences as attitudes and with preference changes as attitude changes. Chapter 13 is somewhat speculative; it discusses using food as psychotherapy and contains proposals for future research.

PART 1

Food: Its Psychological Meaning and Significance

CHAPTER 1

The Role of Food and Eating in Personality and Social Development

Of all the activities in which we normally engage on a daily basis, eating and the psychological effects of food have been almost totally ignored by psychologists. Yet the acquisition and consumption of food is never far from the thoughts of most individuals, even those in affluent societies. Indeed, for many persons, the sole reason for work is to provide food, clothing, shelter, and essential services for themselves and their families. Except for taxes and shelter, food claims the largest part of their incomes. Accurate estimates are difficult to make because of differences in family composition and income levels. The United States Department of Labor no longer publishes itemized family budget expenditures, but in 1981 it reported that a metropolitan-area family of four with an intermediate income spent the following percents of its total income on the three household categories: food, 23 percent; housing, 22 percent; clothing, 5 percent. A lower-income family spent 30 percent of its income on food, while a higher-income family spent 19 percent (*Statistical Abstracts of the United States* 1982). In a 1986 survey of its readers, *Consumer Reports* obtained comparable figures for a roughly equivalent family: food, 20 percent; housing, 24 percent; and clothing, 5 percent (*Consumer Reports* 1986). In 1984, 15 percent of the average after-tax income was spent on food (*Family Economic Review* 1986). Of this, approximately 28 percent was spent for food prepared outside the home. By late 1985, that figure had risen to 40 percent (*CKO News* 1985), with 22 percent of the meals being eaten away from home and 25 percent of the food dollar being spent on those meals (*Restaurants and Institutions* 1985).

3

Food in Daily Living
Childhood

The amount of income spent on food does not, however, give full weight to the importance placed on food throughout our lives, particularly during our formative years when food is given to us without our sharing in the responsibility for obtaining it. First, there is the process of training, when we are ordered, cajoled, threatened, bribed, and in other ways bamboozled into acquiring good manners or eating what is good for us simply because someone bigger than we are says we should. We are told to eat nicely and not make a mess; or to eat so we will grow big and strong; or not to eat foods that will rot our teeth or make us obese. If we won't eat the cold mashed squash set before us, it is implied that we must somehow bear the guilt for the starving millions of the world. When parents pretend the food is really delicious, they begin to establish the child's realization that they are not always truthful. These early years are a hodgepodge of *do*'s and *don't*s. Nutritional requirements are hopelessly confused with the niceties of eating as imposed or expected by one's family and the culture in which one lives. The point is not that either of these considerations should be abandoned, but rather that food plays a dominant and confusing role in our growing up.

Adolescence

As we enter our teens the direct emphasis on food continues unabated. We are told we are getting fat from eating hamburgers and french fries, or that our skin problems are caused by eating candy bars instead of fresh fruit. In fact, today's teenagers are probably given as many dire warnings about the adverse effects of food as their parents were given about the adverse effects of sex.

It is also during the teens that food takes on a subtle role in our orientation toward the future. Teenagers are admonished to prepare for earning a living, to give thought to "putting food on the table." The emphasis on food may be indirect in these considerations of the future, but it is nonetheless pervasive and persistent. The choice of a career, the selection of a mate, and our general lifestyles are affected by associations between food and various attitudes implanted in us intentionally or unintentionally by those around us.

Adulthood

Although Americans like to think of themselves as a classless society, social mobility in the United States is largely constrained by table manners, food preferences, and familiarity with various kinds of foods. If we prefer meat loaf to lobster, we are thought to lack "class." If we ask for corned

1. GRADE **A** SALMON
   or (TUNA)
   ↓
   (CAN BE EATEN RAW,)
   & WILL BE.

2. **10** ZUCHINNI SQUASH, CARROTS
   CUCUMBERS.

3. **7** HEADS BOK CHOY LETTUCE

4. **1 ql** SOIL SAUCE

5. **½ ql** RICE WINE

6. **4** .75lt BOTTLES of SAKE

7. **6 lb** SHORT GRAIN RICE

8. **½ lb** SEA SALT

9. **8 oz** SESAMI SEEDS

10. **1** .75lt BOTTLE of SESAMI OIL

11. **3** WHOLE GINGERS (ROOT)

12. **2 lb** GREEN TEA

13. **2** BOXES of DRY SEA WEED.

14. **1 lb** CRAB MEAT.

15. **3** WHOLE SPRIGS of DILL.

16. **5** EGGS

GROCERIES 3/20
FOR PRIVATE PARTY

SUSHI APPETIZERS

→ 1. STEAM RICE TO STICKY TEXTURE
2. SLIGHTLY MOISTEN SEA WEED SHEET
3. COVER SHEET 3/4 ↓ IN 1/4" THICKNESS.
4. ROLL W/ INSIDE TUNA/CRAB.

SALAD:
1. JULLIAN ALL VEGGIE'S
2. 1/8" CUBE TUNA (RAW)
3. BOK CHOY LAYER PLATE
4. TOSS VEGGIE'S, TUNA. PINCH SALT
   SESAMI OIL, SOY SAUCE, RICE WINE
5. GARNISH WITH SESAMI SEEDS, PEPPER
   GREEN ONION SPRIGS

ENTREE: (.

beef hash or a macaroni-and-cheese casserole in an exclusive restaurant, we embarrass our companions, and even though we actually order Beef Wellington, the waiter snubs us or serves us condescendingly for the rest of the evening. Anyone who likes liver is either odd or anemic, and anyone who drinks buttermilk is thought to be aging, dull, and constipated. A male who does not like steak or roast beef is seen as somewhat less than red-blooded and would certainly be considered a poor marriage risk by many girls' parents. Until recently, one might have been taunted with ethnic slurs for liking Polish sausage, provolone cheese, or catfish. Ethnic foods, however, have become popular and chic, and many foods that were once considered déclassé now appeal to people. In order to be socially correct, one must keep up with these changes. Quiche is a bit passé, while the lowly pot roast may be coming into vogue. We are expected to know a variety of fancy foods. Only the unsophisticated would admit to being unfamiliar with Eggs Benedict or Blanquette de Veau. Persons will go without wine in a restaurant rather than run the risk of being classed as gauche by making a "mistake" in ordering or by ordering the wine they like rather than the wine that is "right."

As adults, most of us spend at least two hours a day in eating or preparing to eat. At no time is the thought of food far from our minds. If thoughts of food are not initiated by hunger or habit, they are triggered off by advertisements in magazines and newspapers and on radio and television. The commercials either insist that we eat or assure us that we will have heartburn, acid stomach, and the embarrassment of loose dentures as a consequence of eating. By rights, psychiatrists' couches should be sagging under the weight of clients seeking therapy for food-induced neuroses.

Food and Socialization
Learning Theory

Food is a basic biological need. Without it no one can survive. Because it is a vital necessity, food plays a major role in our socialization. According to *learning theory,* personality and all complex social behavior depend on how one's hunger drive is met and satisfied during one's formative years. In this view, whatever is present when hunger is reduced can itself come to reduce hunger. Holding or cradling a hungry infant tends to alleviate hunger because the infant was previously held or cradled while being fed. Now the infant begins to relax and coo even before beginning to suckle the breast or bottle.

The ways in which hunger is reduced are even more important determiners of personality and may become deep-seated goals in their own right. If the parents drop everything to feed the infant at the slightest sign of distress, he or she may grow up to be selfish and demanding. If the child is fed only when neat, clean, and orderly, he or she will come to value neatness and orderliness.

The needs for approval, recognition, dominance, or security become personal goals and part of one's personality if these things are given or encouraged when hunger is reduced. At another level, the needs for money, position, and power develop because they are in some way associated with food and the reduction of hunger. They may represent a guarantee that food can always be obtained and that hunger will never be a problem. Many lower animals hoard food; chimpanzees will hoard poker chips if they can be used to "buy" food. Among humans, food hoarding usually occurs only under exceptional circumstances, but the hoarding of money is much more common. The hoarding of worthless objects such as old newspapers, bottles, boxes, and even trash may be based on a need for security and some pathological fear associated with childhood hunger.

Psychoanalysis

Sigmund Freud, the founder of psychoanalysis, also suggested that food and the social conditions and parental behavior surrounding eating are important personality determiners. He believed that children go through a series of developmental stages during which stimulation of different parts of the body is the major source of pleasure and satisfaction. One of these is the *oral stage,* which begins at birth and lasts through weaning. The early part of this stage is known as the *oral sucking stage.* During this period, stimulation of the mouth, particularly by sucking, is the greatest source of pleasure. During the latter part of the oral stage—the *oral biting stage*—pleasure is derived from sucking and biting. This corresponds to the weaning period and may represent hostility and aggression directed against withdrawal of the breast or bottle.

Freud believed that it was important not to rush the child through either of these stages (or the later *anal* and *phallic* stages) and that the need for stimulation of the mouth should be fully satisfied. Failure to satisfy the need could result in "fixation" so that the child, even as an adult, would engage in activities to try to make up for the pleasure of which he or she had been deprived.

Of course, if one of the stages were prolonged and a child obtained too much pleasure, he or she would be reluctant to go on to the next stage and fixation could also occur. These fixations would result in the type of adult personality for which stimulation of the mouth, either actual or symbolic, plays a major role.

The oral sucking personality tends to be passive and dependent, like the infant prior to weaning. These persons may be very talkative and go into professions requiring verbal skills. They may be thumb-suckers or overeaters who also drink or smoke too much.

The oral biting personality has many of the same traits. Like the child at weaning, these persons feel highly dependent but also feel resentful at being deprived of the breast or bottle. They may become nail-biters with a tendency to overeat or overdrink. They also tend to be verbally hostile and aggressive and to enjoy the use of sarcasm and biting remarks.

Food and the Control of Others

Food often becomes a weapon both offensive and defensive. It is part of our armature of power and control. It is used as reward or withheld as punishment in order to induce compliance not only in children but in other intimates and friends as well. The special dinner out is conferred as a gift, perhaps even to create an obligation. As young children we were given sweets and desserts to cheer us up, and in later life we may seek their solace in depression.

Just as the parent controls the child, the child controls the parent by accepting or rejecting what is being offered or by eating in a manner desired by the parents. The parent says, "If you are good, you can have dessert," and the child thinks, "If *you* are good, I'll eat the food—if not, I won't." Unpleasant though it may be, this resistance to parental demands is not entirely undesirable. It helps establish the child's concept of self— the awareness that he or she is a separate person with needs, wishes, desires, and a separate will. It lessens the child's sense of dependency, while the child also learns cooperation.

Psychological Research

It is clear that food plays a very important part in our psychological as well as biological growth. The number of food associations we develop over the years is enormous. The thoughts, images, ideas, feelings, and even full-fledged emotions evoked by food touch on every aspect of our conscious and unconscious mental life. It is surprising, therefore, that psychologists have paid so little attention to the development of food preferences and to the psychological effects of food and food-related activities.

Of the many books published on food there is practically nothing on the psychology of food, although there are a few books on related topics (see, for example, Barker 1982; Galler 1984; Logue 1986; Miller 1981; Serban 1975).

Psychologists have spent a great deal of time and effort studying the psychological aspects of work but very little time studying the reasons for working in the first place—the provision of food and shelter. There is abundant and redundant research on vocational choice, career selection, job satisfaction, morale, work efficiency, personnel selection, management training, and the like (Neff 1985). The reason for working, from the worker's point of view, is left unstudied even though some psychologists estimate that as many as 70 percent of the working population are dissatisfied with their jobs and approximately 30 percent wish they had chosen some other line of work. Almost no one sees work as an end or goal in itself.

Of the food, clothing, and shelter trilogy, clothing and shelter have fared somewhat better than food at the hands of psychologists. There have been numerous books and studies on the psychological effects of clothing on the self concept and on the effects of clothing on the impressions others form of us (Ryan 1966). With regard to shelter, psychologists have been interested in environmental planning and the phenomenon of crowding (Baum et al. 1978; Freedman 1975; Zeisel 1981). A small group of psychologists is researching the subtle effects produced on psychic functioning and social behavior by the characteristics of rooms, light, color schemes, furniture arrangements, and the like (Bennett 1977; Birren 1969; Sommer 1969, 1974).

Recently, nutritionists, psychologists with dietary interests, and others have studied the physiological effects of nutrition on psychological functioning. Indeed, this is currently an area of burgeoning interest to professionals and laymen alike (Cheraskin et al. 1976; Galler 1984; Miller 1981; Pearson and Pearson 1976; Serban 1975, Watson 1972). Studies have ranged from the role of sugar in the development of depression to the use of megavitamins in the treatment of schizophrenia (Dufty 1975; Pauling and Hawkins 1980). This kind of research is of tremendous importance, but whether it will produce significant results that can be applied practically remains to be seen. Those studies, however, are primarily biological or physiological rather than psychological, because they are concerned with the physiological effects of food on psychological functioning.

Home economists, cooks, gourmets, and hosts and hostesses have long been aware of the aesthetics of dining—particularly the importance of food combinations and the way in which they are served. Almost every cookbook or menu planner mentions the basic appeal of appearance, flavor, and texture and the roles these qualities play in the overall mood created by a meal.

A Psychology of Food

It is the purpose of this book to undertake a discussion of food and food preferences from the standpoint of general psychology. Although little information is available that bears directly on the specific problems, it is possible to outline a general framework for a psychology of food and to present a point of view that takes into consideration the details already known regarding the nature and content of conscious experience and the complexity of thoughts, images, ideas, and feelings.

This knowledge, combined with a knowledge regarding the development of associations and a knowledge of food as a complex physical stimulus for the evocation of sensory experience, memories, thoughts, images, and feelings, will give a picture of the role of food in our mental life. It will also lay a groundwork so that individuals can discover the meaning and significance that particular foods have for them personally. With this information, it might be possible for individuals to guide and direct memories, recollections, feelings, and mental activities and contents by the foods that are served or selected. Which foods and food combinations enhance the enjoyment of food? Which engender or enhance particular moods, feelings, and attitudes? Which evoke pleasant or painful memory associations? Which improve a person's mental outlook generally? A psychology of food, dealing with these questions, may lead to possible applications for modifying emotions and outlooks.

PART 2
Food Preferences

CHAPTER 2

Long-term Food Preferences

What foods do we like, and why do we like some foods and dislike others? The commonsense answer to the latter question is that it has to do with taste—some foods taste good, and others do not—but, like many commonsense answers, this one is inadequate. It cannot explain why a given food tastes good one day but not another, or why a given food tastes good when served with one thing but not when served with something else. Why did we choose baked salmon for dinner last night when we could have picked any one of a dozen main dishes, and why at the same restaurant did we decide on a veal cutlet the time before? Why do we never eat liver and rarely refuse roast beef?

Some food preferences are stable and fixed over time. They are relatively permanent and unaffected by changes in settings or moods. We like green peas, mashed potatoes, and lamb chops, and we dislike squash, steamed rice, and fried clams. Other preferences are transitory and change from day to day. A breakfast of scrambled eggs and muffins was delightful today but yesterday we wanted French toast and tomorrow it may be cereal and fruit. Even the snacks we choose are not fixed. We may never eat an orange, but one time we may snack on an apple and another time on a candy bar—and then it may not be the same candy bar each time. There are also transitory cravings that come and go.

Clearly, the question of what foods are preferred involves two separate issues. One has to do with the conditions determining whether we like or dislike a particular food. The other has to do with differences between fixed preferences and fluctuating ones—between preferences that last a lifetime and those that change from day to day—and with food selection as well.

The terms *liking* and *preference* are not used consistently in the literature. Sometimes they are used interchangeably. At other times, *preference* is used only when a choice is available: we may like both salmon and halibut, but prefer salmon to halibut either sometimes, usually, or always. The latter is a fixed or stable preference; in the literature liking salmon and disliking halibut is also called a preference. The present chapter deals primarily with liking versus disliking, but since many of the variables associated with liking are also associated with stable or long-term food preferences, a distinction between the two is not always made.

Liked and Disliked Foods

Fluctuations in food preferences are discussed in the next chapter. Some stable preferences are shown in tables 2-1 and 2-2. The results are from two of the most extensive food-preference surveys. The data in table 2-1 were collected in 1972 from almost 3900 enlisted personnel in the U.S. Armed Forces (Meiselman and Waterman 1978). The data in table 2-2 were collected in 1966–1967 from 50,000 students in approximately 200 colleges and universities (Einstein and Hornstein 1970). There may have been some changes in preferences since the studies due to the public's current familiarity with a wider variety of foods and greater awareness of nutritional needs, but the results conform quite well with information available in restaurant-trade magazines such as *Restaurants and Institutions* (formerly *Institutions/Volume Feeding*).

Liking and Disliking

There are some foods we really dislike and would never eat, except to stave off starvation, regardless of how, when, or where they were served. There are others we would eat if served to us, but only to avoid embarrassment to ourselves or others or to convince our children that these foods should be eaten. Finally, there are a few foods we usually dislike but occasionally enjoy at certain times or places. If we dislike a food at all, we almost always dislike it.

With liked foods the situation is somewhat different. Although there are foods of which we are very fond, none of us would want them exclusively day after day. Liking is affected by a variety of influences. These include the time and context in which the food is served as well as personal considerations such as our degree of hunger, our mood at the time (Lyman 1982a; 1982b), and the time elapsed since we last ate the food (Rolls et al. 1981).

Liking and disliking are at opposite ends of the same continuum—one is pleasant and the other is unpleasant—and we might expect the same principles to apply to both, but there seem to be fundamental differences between the two responses.

TABLE 2-1. **High- and low-preference foods of Armed Forces personnel**

Food Class	High-preference	Low-preference
1. Appetizers		
2. Soups	Tomato vegetable noodle soup	Corn chowder
		Fish chowder
	Tomato soup	Split pea soup
	Chicken noodle soup	Egg drop soup
		Onion soup
		Creole soup
3. Fruit and vegetable juices	Orange juice	Cranberry juice
	Grape juice	Prune juice
4. Fruit drinks and iced tea	Lemonade	Grape lemonade
	Iced tea	Lime-flavored drink
		Cherry-flavored drink
5. Hot beverages		Instant coffee
		Freeze-dried coffee
6. Milk products	Milk	Skim milk
	Ice cream	Buttermilk
		Fruit-flavored yogurt
7. Carbonated beverages	Cola	Low-calorie soda
9. Hot bread and doughnuts	Doughnuts	
	Sweet breads	Plain muffins
10. Breakfast cereals	Cold cereal	
11. Griddle cakes	Griddle cakes	
12. Eggs		
13. Breakfast meats	Bacon	Grilled bologna
	Canadian bacon	Scrapple
14. Fish and seafood	French fried shrimp	Baked fish
	Seafood platter	Salmon
	Lobster	Baked tuna and noodles
15. Meats	Roast beef	Grilled lamb chops
	Swiss steak	Spareribs with sauerkraut
	Pot roast	Corned beef
	Grilled steak	Pork hocks
	Grilled minute steak	Pickled pigs' feet
	Barbecued spareribs	Sauerbraten
	Grilled ham	
	Baked ham	
	Italian sausage	
	Fried chicken	
	Baked chicken	
	Hot turkey sandwich with gravy	
	Hot roast beef sandwich with gravy	

continued

TABLE 2-1. **High- and low-preference foods of Armed Forces personnel**
(continued)

Food Class	High-preference	Low-preference
16. Stews and extended meats	Lasagna Pizza Spaghetti with meat sauce Spaghetti and meat balls Meatloaf Swedish meat balls Salisbury steak Beef stew	Chicken cacciatore Chili macaroni Ham loaf Vealburger Stuffed cabbage Corn beef hash Stuffed green peppers Pork chop suey Sweet and sour pork Sukiyaki Baked tuna and noodles
17. Short order, sandwiches	Hamburger Cheeseburger Ham sandwich Bacon, lettuce, and tomato sandwich Grilled cheese sandwich Grilled ham and cheese sandwich Sloppy Joe Pizza	Frankfurter, cheese, and bacon Salami sandwich Bologna sandwich Hot Reuben sandwich Hot pastrami sandwich Fishwich
18. Potato and potato substitutes	French fried potatoes Baked potatoes Hashed brown potatoes Mashed potatoes Potato chips	Sweet potatoes Hot potato salad Boiled navy beans Refried beans Rice pilaf Cornbread stuffing Savory bread stuffing Sausage stuffing
19. Green vegetables	Canned green beans Frozen green beans Canned peas Collard greens Buttered mixed vegetables	Frozen lima beans Canned lima beans Creamed frozen peas Fried cabbage Brussels sprouts Mustard greens Turnip greens Butter zucchini squash
20. Yellow vegetables	Cream-style corn Corn-on-the-cob Buttered whole-kernel corn	Baked yellow squash French fried carrots
21. Other vegetables	French fried onion rings	Mashed rutabagas Fried parsnips

continued

TABLE 2-1. **High- and low-preference foods of Armed Forces personnel** (continued)

Food Class	High-preference	Low-preference
22. Fruit salads	Mixed fruit salad	Pineapple cheese salad
23. Vegetable salads	Cole slaw	Pickled beet and onion
	Celery and carrot sticks	salad
		Carrot, raisin, and celery salad
		Kidney bean salad
24. Tossed green salads		
25. Salad dressings	Thousand Island dressing	Sour cream dressing
	French dressing	Blue cheese
26. Fresh fruit	Oranges	Plums
	Apples	Honeydew melon
		Fruit cup
27. Canned fruits	Peaches	Plums
	Pears	Apricots
	Applesauce	Figs
	Fruit cocktail	Stewed prunes
28. Cookies and brownies	Chocolate chip cookies	Molasses cookies
	Peanut butter cookies	Coconut raisin
	Chocolate cookies	Fruit bars
	Oatmeal cookies	Nut bars
	Brownies	Butterscotch brownies
29. Cakes	Strawberry shortcake	Spice cake
	Pineapple upside-down cake	White cake
	Devil's food cake	Peanut butter cake
	Banana cake	Yellow cake
		Cheesecake
		Gingerbread
30. Pies	Cherry pie	Raisin pie
	Apple pie	Pineapple pie
	Pumpkin pie	Apricot pie
	Strawberry chiffon pie	Pineapple cream pie
	Banana cream pie	Sweet potato pie
	Lemon meringue pie	
31. Pudding and other desserts	Chocolate pudding	Bread pudding
	Banana cream pudding	Rice pudding
	Apple crisp	Fruit-flavored yogurt
32. Ice cream and sherbet	Ice cream	Butterscotch sundae
	Milk shake	Pineapple sundae

Reprinted from: Meiselman, H. L. and Waterman, D. (1978). Food preferences of enlisted personnel in the armed forces. *Journal of the American Dietetic Association*, 73: 621–29.

TABLE 2.2. **The 10 percent of all surveyed foods best and least liked by college students**

Best liked		Least liked	
Percent liked	Menu item	Percent disliked	Menu item
94	Ice cream	68	Sautéed chicken livers
94	Soft rolls	66	Turnips
92	Beef steak	62	Sautéed liver
92	Hot biscuits	61	French fried eggplant
92	Milk	58	Cabbage
92	Orange juice	58	Pickled beets
91	Roast turkey	57	Baked squash
90	Roast beef	57	Stewed tomatoes
89	Apple pie	56	Carrot-raisin salad
89	Fried chicken	56	Stewed rhubarb
89	Ice cream sundae	54	Stewed prunes
89	Strawberry shortcake	53	Cream cheese and jelly sandwich
88	Doughnuts	53	Navy bean soup
88	French fried potatoes	52	Cucumber and onion salad
88	Hamburger	51	Cauliflower
88	Sliced peaches	51	Soft-cooked eggs
87	Chocolate chip cookies	49	Stuffed pepper
87	Fruit cup	48	Brussels sprouts
86	Brownies	48	Lamb stew
86	Tossed green salad	48	Succotash
		48	Sauerkraut

Reprinted by permission from: Einstein, M. A. and Hornstein, I. (1970). Food preferences of college students and nutritional implications. *Journal of Food Science*, 35: 429–35. Copyright © by Institute of Food Technologists.

Qualitative Differences in Experiences

Qualitative differences in positive and negative experiences are found in other areas of psychology. For example, the patterns of thoughts and images are different in pleasant and unpleasant emotions (Lyman 1984). There are more imageless thoughts during unpleasant emotions, and the thinking is more tied to the situation that arouses the emotion. In pleasant emotions there is more imagery; the thoughts and images are less tied to the situation and are more likely to evoke other thoughts and images to form a sequence or chain of images resulting in flights of the imagination.

First Impressions

First impressions—whether of situations, objects, or people—color all subsequent later ones and, therefore, they are particularly important (Asch

1946, 1952). Our first impressions of a person may later prove false, but initially we tend to see what a person does in a way that fits in with the initial impression. Later impressions tend to be distorted so as to confirm the first impression. If we think someone is selfish, on the basis of our first meeting, we will tend to see selfishness in all of his or her future actions. Or we may excuse apparently selfish behavior in someone who we perceived to be unselfish on our first meeting on the grounds that the person wasn't feeling well that day.

Positive and negative impressions differ psychologically. A single negative experience seems to have a stronger and more lasting effect than a single positive one. If we have had a bad experience with a person, we are likely to dislike the person forever and actively avoid having any contact with him or her. A single positive experience, however, does not necessarily lead to our actively seeking the person out. The same principle applies to food preferences. A single negative experience may result in a lasting aversion, while a single positive one has a less pronounced positive effect (Garb and Stunkard 1974).

The order of the impressions is also important. If the first impression is negative but all subsequent experiences with the person are positive, we may slowly change our opinion and decide the person is good or kind after all. However, if this series of positive encounters is followed by one new negative encounter, months or even years later, we are likely to revert quickly to our original view and say to ourselves, "I should have known better; I didn't think he was any good the first time I met him, and I was right all the time." On the other hand, if a positive first impression is followed by a series of unpleasant experiences, the initial impression probably changes quite quickly to a negative one, and a single positive experience subsequently does not make us revert to our original impression, no matter how strong it was.

The same principles apply to our reactions to food. If positive experiences follow an initial negative one, we continue to be skeptical and cautious, and if there is now one bad experience, we quickly revert to our original impression. Similarly, a whole series of pleasant experiences can be quickly scuttled by a single unpleasant one.

Finally, whether we like or dislike someone on the first meeting seems to be based on different aspects of the person (Lyman et al. 1981). Positive and negative first impressions are both correlated with liking or disliking the person's physical characteristics—face, hair, eyes, and so forth. Liking is also correlated with liking the person's behavior—what he is doing or how he does it—and with how we imagine the person would behave in other situations. Disliking is not significantly related to either of these responses. There are similarities here with food preferences. In the chapter on associations and food meanings it is pointed out that there are more associations referring to the physical characteristics of disliked foods than of liked or neutral foods.

It seems clear that, in psychological terms, liking and disliking differ by more than the simple facts that one is pleasant and the other is unpleasant or that one is favorable and the other is unfavorable. Disliking seems to be more concrete and durable and less easily modified. Liking is more subject to temporary fluctuations and seems to be more influenced by meanings and ideas. For food preferences, this is seen in the fact that liked and disliked foods have associations that are different in kind and not simply in their pleasantness or unpleasantness.

Just how and to what extent the facts of pleasant and unpleasant emotions and the general principles of liking and disliking in the impressions we form of individuals apply to food preferences is not entirely clear. Some suggestions have been made above and other possibilities will be discussed later. However, since there are only a few studies directly relating psychological principles to food preferences, any conclusions are somewhat tentative and are in need of confirmation by further research.

Variables Related to Stable Food Preferences

A great many variables affecting food preferences have been identified. Some of these are given in table 2-3. The list is representative rather than exhaustive, and for some of the variables contradictory results have been reported. There are other difficulties in compiling such a list. Many researchers investigate the influence of several variables at once, and these may interact so that any one variable has no direct effect by itself, but

TABLE 2-3. **Some representative variables associated with long-term food preferences**

Food characteristics (Hertzler 1983; Todhunter 1973; Tuorila-Ollikainen and Mahlamaki-Kultanen 1985)
Body weight (Blackman et al. 1983; Cinciripini 1984)
Age (Moskowitz 1978b; Pilgrim 1961)
Sex or race (Tuorila-Ollikainen and Mahlamaki-Kultanen 1985; Wyant and Meiselman 1984)
Self-concept (George and Krondl 1983; Schafer 1979)
Socioeconomic status (Sexton 1974)
Peer or other models (Birch 1980b; Escalona 1945)
Parental attitudes (Yperman and Vermeersch 1979)
Family relations (Rozin et al. 1984; Schafer and Keith 1978)
Nutrition knowledge (Dubbert et al. 1984; Grotkowski and Sims 1978)
Television viewing (Goldberg et al. 1978; Jeffrey et al. 1982)
Familiarity (Birch 1979b, 1980a, 1981; Birch and Marlin 1982; Pliner 1982)
Context (Birch et al. 1980; Douglas 1979; Pilgrim 1961)
Geography (Katz 1982; Pilgrim 1961; Simoons 1983)
Culture (Kandel et al. 1980; Paul 1955)
Food meanings (Gifft et al. 1976; Krondl et al. 1982)

becomes important in conjunction with some other variable(s). For example, sex and age interact. There are no sex differences in food preferences among the very young, but they become apparent in older children. An additional problem has to do with how preferences are measured. Sometimes it is simply a matter of asking whether a particular food is liked or disliked, but one cannot always rely on the accuracy of the answers. Most people tend to give favorable answers more freely than unfavorable ones. In some studies, eating is taken as an indication of preference, and although the correlation between what foods are preferred and what foods are eaten is sometimes fairly good, sometimes it is not. There are many reasons why one eats foods that may or may not be the preferred ones, and therefore eating cannot be taken as a sure sign of preference. The studies cited in table 2-3 are all good ones, and nothing above is meant to detract from them, but the reader should keep in mind that the researchers may have qualified their findings.

Unlearned and Specifically Learned Food Preferences
Unlearned Preferences

Our very first encounter with food involves taste, temperature, texture, and smell; almost universally it is mother's milk or a facsimile thereof, and most infants show an immediate liking for it. Is this, as well as other preferences, innate, or are preferences acquired through a variety of complex processes?

Flavor and texture: Liquids and soft foods seem to be innately preferred, and infants will not willingly accept solid foods much before they are ten weeks old. Even though the first "solid" foods are soft and bland and do not differ greatly in flavor characteristics, parents report the appearance of preferences at this early age. Since this is the child's first introduction to a variety of foods, there has been little or no opportunity for learning to occur or for complex meanings to develop. Therefore, it is reasonable to conclude that the preferences are innate and based on some flavor and texture differences, even though they are very subtle. (As discussed later, it is possible, but unlikely, that tissue needs play a role.)

These early preferences and aversions do not mean that there are innate preferences for specific foods, but rather for certain sensory qualities which various foods have. We are not born liking butterscotch pudding and disliking spinach. Rather, we have a preference for the sweetness of pudding and an aversion to the bitterness of spinach.

Evidence suggests that even mother's milk as such has no strongly preferred status, other than its sweetness (Desor et al. 1973). On a short-term basis, sweetened liquids lacking nutritional value are taken as often. In fact, the infant may prefer sweetened water to milk.

Adaptive values: Humans, like many lower animals, seem to have an inborn preference for sweet substances and an aversion to sour and bitter ones (Beidler 1983). This may have some adaptive value since many bitter substances are poisonous while most naturally sweet ones are not. There also appear to be innate preferences and aversions in odor, but—as with all the senses—we cannot be certain, since such conclusions are based on fairly undifferentiated facial expressions the newborn infant makes when chemical substances are presented. A conservative conclusion is that the newborn distinguishes at least some pleasant and unpleasant stimuli by making accepting or rejecting responses.

Food meanings: The chemical senses form the earliest bases for human food preferences. Soon afterward, appearance begins to play a role as form and color become associated with taste and smell and the hunger-reducing properties of food. Some time later, during the child's first year, food begins to take on complex meanings signifying comfort and security, activities and events. Later, food gathers still more complex meanings. Bacon means breakfast; cake means birthdays; popcorn means movies; and macaroni and cheese can mean that we have run out of money. These meanings, rather than the physical characteristics of the foods, become increasingly important, and by the time we are teenagers they may be the most important determiners of our food preferences and selections.

Learned Food Preferences

With the introduction of solid foods, served at different times and in different combinations and places, the ground is laid for the acquisition of a variety of different likes and dislikes. Some of these preferences are specifically learned. According to learning theory, we may come to like a particular food because it, rather than some other food, was used to reduce hunger. Or we may come to like the food because we were rewarded in other ways, such as by praise or sweets, for eating it.

Reward does not ensure liking: According to learning theory, if we had been fed pureed grubs rather than pureed chicken when hungry, we would have grown up liking grubs and being indifferent to chicken. That may be true; grubs are a delicacy in some cultures. There are, however, several flaws to the theory. Thousands of children are fed pureed liver. It reduces hunger and is nutritionally valuable. Those same thousands are also rewarded with praise and perhaps with a favored dessert for eating it. Yet among those very thousands are hundreds who will grow up to detest liver. Most of them will do so even though it never made them ill, they were never forced to eat it, and no great unpleasant issue was made of their not eating it. Even with positive rewards and no negative experiences to make the food unacceptable, it will still be disliked. Traditional learning theory is predicated on the assumption that any object can come to be desired if appropriate rewards are given, but it fails to consider the fact that the object may have characteristics that set limits on or outweigh the effectiveness of rewards. In some individuals, for example, the sense of taste might cause them to detect a slight bitterness in liver; or their odor sensitivity might make the smell unpleasant; or they may find the texture disagreeable.

Foods used as rewards come to be liked: In two recent studies of preschool-age children, one group was allowed access to a favorite play activity as a reward for drinking a novel juice which was neither liked nor disliked (Birch et al. 1982); the other group received verbal praise or access to a movie as a reward for drinking a novelly flavored but neutral milk drink (Birch et al. 1984). Preferences for the foods actually decreased rather than increased. On the other hand, when neutral but mostly healthful snacks were given as rewards after one of several desirable behaviors, preference for both the sweet and nonsweet snacks increased. Preference for snacks given by the teacher in a friendly manner also increased, but not for those given nonsocially by simply being placed in the child's locker (Birch et al. 1980). Preferences for foods used as rewards increased, but rewards for eating foods did not increase the desirability for those foods.

Given the failure of rewards consistently to produce acquired preferences, it must be concluded that reward can work only when the food falls within the limits of acceptable taste, odor, texture, and appearance, but even then preferences for the food may decrease if obtaining it is seen somehow as dependent on completing some required activity.

Learning occurs without hunger reduction: There are other considerations which suggest that learning does not depend on the hunger-reducing properties of foods. Rats, for example, will learn maze paths when saccharin, which tastes sweet but has no nutritional value, is used as reward. Rats and human infants and adults stop taking in food long before a sufficient amount has been absorbed into the system to alleviate hunger or thirst (Stellar 1954). When hungry or thirsty rats are allowed to eat or drink but the food is directed so that it cannot reach the stomach, the foods still act as rewards and facilitate maze-learning even though there has been no reduction in physiological hunger.

Acquired Food Aversions

For acquired food preferences, the studies cited above suggest that what happens in the mouth is more important than what happens in the stomach. Taste, odor, and texture seem more important than the hunger-reducing properties of food. These are also important in food dislikes (Rozin and Fallon 1980).

With acquired food *aversions,* however, the situation is different. The stomach, not the mouth, is dominant. We may come to dislike a food because it upsets our stomach or because we anticipate some harm from it, but if we like a food, it is because it tastes good and not because it makes our stomach feel good. If a food isn't good in the mouth, we are unlikely to eat it. If we feel upset or become ill after eating a food that tasted neutral or good, an aversion lasting for years may develop because of what happened after the food reached the stomach.

Relatively few food dislikes, as opposed to real aversions, are attributable to an association with actual illness (Pelchat and Rozin 1982). Learned aversions seem to be acquired as conditioned responses; that is, a previously neutral or liked food comes to have negative properties or to be disliked because it was paired with some unpleasant sensory or environmental experience. Some positive preferences may be acquired in the same way, but usually they are learned more subtly, often by our simply being exposed to the foods over time. Many food dislikes also are acquired subtly, with physical and social contexts and attitudes of disgust or contamination being important (Fallon et al. 1984).

Incidentally Acquired Food Preferences

Most food preferences are acquired and are learned indirectly rather than through specific training or intent. We pick up attitudes and beliefs and likes and dislikes, not by choice, but by accident from those around us or from the physical and social world in which we live. This unintentional acquisition is called *incidental learning*. There are several classes of incidental learning, and many of the variables listed in table 2-3 fall into those classes. Among the categories are: familiarity, exposure, and imitation. Novelty and complexity of stimuli as well as personality dispositions also contribute to incidental learning.

Familiarity and Exposure

Social psychologists have shown that simply being exposed to stimuli as diverse as nonsense words, music, paintings, photographs of strangers, and real individuals who are unknown to us results in a more favorable attitude toward them, even though the initial reaction may have been indifference or mild aversion (Zajonc 1968). Thus, familiarity breeds liking rather than contempt. Simple exposure enhances preferences and acceptance.

Directly or indirectly, familiarity accounts for many of the variables such as culture or family background, shown in table 2-3, which are correlated with long-term food preferences, and familiarity is listed by many researchers as the single most important determiner of food preferences. We tend to like those foods that are familiar and to ignore or reject those that are not. Low levels of exposure, however, do not result in preference changes (Peryam 1963).

Of course, what is familiar now was at one time unfamiliar. How do unfamiliar foods become familiar? Perhaps the most common way is through exposure to various foods while we are growing up. This exposure may involve foods set before us from our earliest years as well as foods seen in store displays or advertisements. Thus, the millions spent on advertising not only keep the products' names in mind but also foster favorable attitudes toward them. Ordinarily, exposure takes place over an extended period of time, but experiments show that even short-term attention-getting exposure to novel foods increases preferences. The effect occurs in young children (Birch and Marlin 1982) as well as in adults (Pliner 1982). Of course, prolonged exposure to already familiar foods can produce a temporary decrease in preference (Siegel and Pilgrim 1958). This is one of the reasons for fluctuations in preferences. There is less dissatisfaction, however, if individuals have some say in selecting the foods in a monotonous diet (Kamen and Peryam 1961).

Family influences: Whoever or whatever determines the foods we are exposed to also determines our preferences. Until recently, the very earliest influence was the mother or mother substitute—a nurse in wealthy homes or a grandmother or older sister or brother in others. In families where both parents work outside the home, it may be either the mother or father, but in those as well as in single-parent families it is more likely to be a sitter or, a little later, the staff of a day-care center. The family may be losing control of the development of food preferences. As the child gets older, the erosion of family influences increases.

The child used to grow up within a family setting which for reasons of economy, geography, tradition, and choice served certain foods and ignored others. With minimal outside influences until the school-age years, the family was the major source of emerging food preferences. Whether that was nutritionally good or bad depended on the family's eating habits. If green vegetables were never served, the child would not develop a liking for them. On the other hand, if healthy foods were presented, those are the kinds of preferences likely to have developed. So parents who serve a balanced, healthy diet are doing more than simply giving their children a good diet; they are helping to establish nutritionally sound preferences that may last a lifetime.

Influences outside the home: Children's preferences are increasingly influenced by television, by restaurants, and by peers. Up to 40 percent of the family's food dollar is spent on food prepared outside the home (*CKO News* 1985). Restaurants catering to families have become common, and many families or children and their sitters eat out at least once a week. This means that restaurants and what is served there and what children see others eating are factors that increasingly determine food preferences. In many ways this is unfortunate, since it means that family traditions that may have lasted for generations are being lost. In the Pacific Northwest there are still descendants of New Englanders who have baked beans on a wintery Saturday night and who enjoy eating pie for breakfast, but the tradition may be lost in favor of restaurant menus.

Although one may regret the declining family influence, it is possible that people are eating better nutritionally now than they did when the family was more important and most meals were eaten at home. The birthday party with cake and ice cream at home is being replaced by pizza and soda at a restaurant. The pizza is certainly more nutritious. An evening snack of cookies, fudge, or popcorn is replaced by a hamburger, french fries, and soda. Again, the latter meal is more nutritious. Fast foods are much maligned. True, they are high in calories, are usually eaten at a pace unfavorable for digestion, and—if eaten exclusively—may preclude a more balanced intake, but they are not unhealthy. As usually served, they are deficient in dairy products and high in fat content, but the hamburger often contains some lettuce, the pizza has tomato, and the fried chicken comes with potato salad or cole slaw.

There is another positive side to the changing role of family values. With food commercials everywhere, a fast-food restaurant on almost every commercial corner, and specialty shops and delicatessens almost as frequent, we are being exposed to a much greater variety of foods than ever before. If the familiarity-preference hypothesis is correct, this means the development of a much broader range of preferences than in the past, and the more variety in one's diet, the greater the chances of eating a balanced diet. However, this exposure to diversity is counteracted to some extent by the fact that our culture is becoming more homogenous. McDonald's is everywhere, and geographical distance no longer isolates or preserves subcultures. Differences are disappearing under the impact of mass communication.

Evaluation of the familiarity-preference hypothesis: Familiarity seems to foster liking, but is simple exposure to foods enough to make us like them? Probably not. The context or setting in which exposure takes place is important. It must be either neutral or positive. A negative setting or context can create an unfavorable attitude. For example, in person perception, the meaning of a single personality trait is determined by the other traits present (Asch 1952). Industriousness is seen as good when it occurs with friendliness, generosity, kindness, and honesty, but as negative when it occurs with unfriendliness, selfishness, cruelty, and deceit. In the same way, a neutral or even moderately liked food can come to have a negative meaning if it occurs in association with poverty or uncleanliness, or if it is served or eaten by persons whom we dislike or for whom we have little or no respect.

Exposure in a neutral setting may produce liking, but favorable attitudes are most effectively created by a positive context, and one of the most effective positive contexts is one in which there is some element of prestige—seeing the food in an opulent setting or seeing it enjoyed by one's peers, one's television heroes, or even one's parents. For young children, adults obviously have prestige or there would be no games such as playing house or pretending to be grown up. Even rebellious teenagers respect some of their parents' opinions and may even come to tell them so one day.

Finally, for foods to be liked, they have to be tried. One can dislike foods, or at least refuse them because of their appearance or the particular meanings associated with them, without tasting them. Seeing a food or seeing someone eat it may make one want to try it, but that is not the same as liking it. People buy or try many things they think they would like only to find out they don't. (How many useless kitchen gadgets are bought each year?) Once tried, the actual taste of a food can override a preference established by exposure and familiarity.

Novelty

A common feeding problem with children is getting them to try new foods. This resistance to accepting the unfamiliar is evident as early as the shift from liquids to solid foods. The resistance may be due in part to disliking the taste, flavor, and textures of the new foods, but it is also due in part to their strangeness. Whether the child's taste has become adapted to certain flavors and textures so that new ones actually "taste" unpleasant is difficult to ascertain, since the child's grimacing and other signs of displeasure could be aroused by either taste or unfamiliarity. Verbal statements, even from older children, can be ambiguous. "It doesn't taste good" could be a literal statement or it could simply mean the child doesn't like the food.

The psychological evidence regarding novelty is conflicting. On the one hand, new or novel stimuli seem to evoke tension, fear, or apprehension. Fear of the unknown is well documented, whether it involves a simple stimulus or something more complex such as speaking before a group of strangers or starting a new job.

Some psychologists have suggested that a child's fear of the dark comes about after the child has learned that the world is full of identifiable objects and people. In the dark, none of the amorphous shapes or sounds is familiar. Thus, fear of the dark is due to the absence of the familiar rather than the presence of the unfamiliar. The gradual transition from liquid to semiliquid to soft to solid foods may be proper not only physiologically but also psychologically because it prevents a sudden change from familiar to unfamiliar.

There is another side to novelty. Laboratory rats have an exploratory drive—a tendency to explore strange and unfamiliar places. In humans new and novel stimuli evoke interest and curiosity. We pay attention to them. Infants explore new objects with their eyes and mouth. Aesthetically, moderate novelty in form or sound is pleasing (Berlyne 1971). Repetition of the familiar—whether in music, painting, or food—becomes boring.

How can these conflicting data—suggesting both fear and interest or avoidance and approach—be reconciled? First, as stated above, moderately novel objects or situations evoke interest and curiosity. If they are too unusual or unfamiliar, they evoke anxiety or fear. Second, curiosity and interest may differ according to which sense is involved. The studies on novelty and curiosity have dealt almost exclusively with visual stimuli. From the standpoint of survival, a cautious interest in the unfamiliar is adaptive when the helpful or harmful qualities of the object or situation are unknown. Seeing an unfamiliar object allows time to find out whether it is harmful, but if it is eaten—or perhaps only tasted—the damage is already done if it is poisonous. Therefore, among young people, there may be greater resistance or neophobia to tastes than to other novel stimuli, and refusing to eat unfamiliar foods could be particularly helpful. This interpretation is supported by the finding that younger children (Birch 1979a) and younger adults (Otis 1984) are less willing than older ones to taste unfamiliar foods.

A third reason why the novelty research with visual stimuli shows both approach and avoidance reactions may be that curiosity and interest in the unfamiliar are more prevalent at one age than at another, although psychologists do not agree on what those ages are (Karl 1974). Certainly they are present in infancy and childhood, as the phrase "childlike curiosity" attests, but the development is not steady. Young infants often prefer familiar stimuli while older infants spend more time looking at novel ones (Fantz 1966). Unfortunately, curiosity seems to decline in adults; in some it almost entirely disappears—or, perhaps, it only becomes dormant. The current rage for exotic fruits and vegetables shows that novelty attracts interest and consumption. Some of this may be due to prestige values. When something becomes fashionable one wants not only to keep up with the Joneses but to excel them as well, perhaps by being the first to serve a new food.

Whatever the reason, as familiarity with novel foods increases so do their acceptance and popularity. Some foods that were ignored or rejected a few years ago are now highly prized (Vietmeyer 1985). Exotic produce has become a lucrative industry, and land devoted to more traditional crops is being converted to its production.

It has been suggested that North America is in the throes of a food revolution much like that in Europe at the time of Columbus, when "exotic" foods of the Western Hemisphere were being introduced. Such foods as tomatoes, squash, potatoes, and corn were rejected at first, but today they are staples. Similarly, many of today's new foods will be commonplace tomorrow.

Imitation

To imitate or copy is a natural tendency which need not depend on conscious intent. It seems to occur automatically and is noticeable, particularly in the young, in a variety of species such as dogs, goats, monkeys, and humans. Its presence is confirmed by the adage "Monkey see, monkey do." Infants as young as thirty-six hours old will imitate the facial expressions of adults (Steiner 1977). The infant's reciprocating response to a smile is familiar to all. Reward, praise, and encouragement may strengthen the tendency to copy or imitate, but they are not necessary for it to occur.

Attitudes as well as behaviors can be conveyed—and often are—by very subtle gestures or facial expressions. In a classic study, juice preferences of babies in a prison nursery changed to fit the preferences of those giving the juice even though those caring for the infants were completely unaware of transmitting any preference cues (Escalona 1945).

In spite of the fact that imitation is universal in humans, psychologists rarely have stressed its importance in the acquisition of behavior and attitudes, perhaps because it is not obvious in rats, upon which much learning theory is based.

Of course, not everyone's behavior is copied. At an early time, perhaps as soon as the child can tell the difference between a stranger and someone familiar, there is a greater likelihood of copying someone who has prestige or who is familiar, respected, or admired. Later there is a tendency to copy the majority so that one does not stand out as different, at least not from the group to which one belongs or wishes to belong.

As already suggested, many of the variables in table 2-3 affect the development of food preferences through familiarity. Others, no doubt, do so through imitation of the preference behaviors of those around us. Perhaps we acquire food preferences most readily by being exposed to foods by those whose attitudes or behaviors we wish to copy.

Personality and Food Preferences

Newspaper and magazine stories often report a relation between specific personality traits or characteristics and specific food preferences. For example, it has been suggested that persons who like hash and casseroles are problem solvers who like complexity, or that adults who like milk have a mother fixation or haven't quite grown up. (Actually the dislike for milk may be due to a genetically determined inability to digest lactose; this occurs in many people when they reach one and one-half to three years of age [Kretchmer 1978]).

Although specific food preferences and specific personality traits may go together, appropriate systematic studies showing such relations have not been reported. Such relations may be discovered through additional research, but it is likely that personality differences affect food preferences in a general way and show up as likes or dislikes for general kinds or classes of foods rather than for specific food items. Several areas of personality study suggest general relations between personality and food preferences. Some of these are discussed below.

Concrete versus Abstract Attitudes

Two questions on one of the standard psychological tests of intelligence are "How are coat and dress alike?" and "How are newspaper and radio alike?" Answers can be given at three different thought levels: (1) a concrete answer that refers to the physical characteristics of the items (both have sleeves; both use words); (2) a functional answer that refers to the use or purpose of the items (both keep you warm; both convey information); or (3) an abstract answer that refers to the general class to which the items belong (both are wearing apparel; both are communications media).

In a different test of active concept formation, a variety of objects is shown (Goldstein and Sheerer 1941). Among them are regular and toy silver cutlery, a padlock, regular and toy hammer and pliers, two nails, two sugar cubes, and a variety of paper and rubber products. The individual is then given one of the objects and asked to pick out all the others that belong with it and to indicate why they belong together. If the fork is presented, a person who thinks at the abstract level might put all cutlery with it. A concrete response might include all shiny objects; a functional response might include all things used for eating. If the hammer is presented, an abstract response might include all tools; a concrete response might include all things made of metal; and a functional response might include all things that can be used in making repairs.

Insofar as these kinds of responses represent personalities with different thought modes, it is reasonable to expect some differences in food preferences. A concrete-minded person would pay more attention to food's physical characteristics, such as taste, odor, texture, and appearance, and make choices based on those characteristics. Some of the research reported in chapter 11 supports this inference and also shows that individuals who are more concerned with physical characteristics have more food dislikes. Functional-minded individuals would show a greater preference for foods that have specific functional values: those that are nutritious, filling, nonfattening, and so forth. The abstract-minded person would be more responsive to the classes to which foods belong and would pay less attention to the characteristics of specific foods within those classes. The classes might be broad, such as main dishes or desserts, or more restricted, such as fish, meat, cakes, or pies. If the abstract-minded person wanted a sandwich, he or she might not really care what kind, whereas the more concrete-minded person might insist on a chicken or Swiss cheese sandwich. Research supports these inferences. Adults tend to think at the abstract level, and most individuals usually like or dislike most foods within a class; that is, a person who likes peas probably likes most vegetables, and a person who dislikes steak is probably not particularly fond of any red meat (Pilgrim and Kamen 1959).

Need for Stimulation

Some individuals seek out new and unusual experiences (Zuckerman 1979). They seem to need extra excitement and often enjoy taking risks. In psychological terms this is known as *sensation-seeking*, with "sensation" referring to sensory stimulation rather than notoriety. It is measured by answers to questions involving choices between high and low activity or between danger and security. An item on one of the scales reads, "I like to try new foods that I have never tasted before." Sensation-seeking has been correlated with several behavior patterns including delinquency. The assumption is that lawbreaking and the danger of being caught give these persons the extra excitement they crave.

Sensation-seeking has also been found to be correlated with food preferences. For example, sensation-seekers prefer spicy, crunchy, and sour foods rather than bland, soft, and sweet ones (Kish and Donnenwerth 1972). Those who consider themselves gourmets also score higher in sensation-seeking (Back and Glasgow 1981). It is reasonable to suppose that sensation-seekers would prefer or at least be interested in trying new, unusual, and exotic foods, but research results have not always borne this out (Otis 1984). Perhaps this is due to minor differences in research procedures which often produce different results. There is also the problem of defining novelty. *Novelty* should mean the unknown, not the untried. Some novel and unfamiliar foods already have such negative connotations that even sensation-seekers would be unwilling to try them. Blood sausage, sautéed brains, and raw fish (before the popularity of sushi bars) are examples. Finally, results obtained from laboratory studies do not always reflect what happens in the real world. One might be more willing to try a new and unusual food during an evening outing with friends than in a cold, impersonal laboratory setting.

Sensitivity to Food Stimuli

There are individual differences in responsiveness to food stimuli. If cookies are left on the table or cheese in the refrigerator, some individuals will leave them alone unless they are hungry, but others will nibble and eat them simply because they are there. This is known as *external responsivity*. It is found in individuals at all weight levels, but is reported more frequently among the obese (Rodin 1980). In externally responsive individuals, the insulin level rises at the sight of food and this increases hunger. There has been some success treating the obese by minimizing their exposure to food stimuli. Little food is kept in the home, and the individuals are encouraged not to read articles discussing food or food preparation, to avoid food advertisements, and to stay away from supermarkets except to buy needed foods and then in very small quantities. "Out of sight, out of mind" seems to reduce food intake for some people.

In addition to differences in general responsiveness to external stimuli, there are also differences in the way individuals respond to various classes of sensory stimuli. Some people like painting better than music; others like poetry better than dance; and some like lyrics better than instrumentals. For others, enjoyment comes not so much from the physical stimuli as from the imagery and associations they evoke. Sights and sounds, words and movements do not affect us all in the same way. With food preferences, appearance is of primary importance to some; for others, flavor matters most; and for still others, preferences may depend on the imagery and associations the food has with other times and places. In the past, modern marketing procedures and customer demands have emphasized appearance and keeping qualities at the expense of flavor. Old varieties of orchard fruits, for example, that had superb flavor but a dull appearance were dropped from sales and production. They are coming into vogue again, along with some highly unattractive exotic produce.

Neatness and Orderliness

Some individuals cannot stand to have foods touching each other on their plates. Often the same persons will eat one food entirely before eating the next one. They proceed methodically and consecutively through what has been presented. This behavior is more common among children than adults, but it can be found at any age. It may be a carry-over from early eating habits when the first foods were fed one after another, or when the parent insisted that one food be finished completely before another was given. If extreme, the behavior is mildly neurotic. According to Freudian theory, it may be due to a rigid toilet training and fixation at the anal retentive stage because neatness and cleanliness were overemphasized. More commonly, compulsive neatness and orderliness may indicate a need for security which is ensured by having everything just so. If everything is orderly and nothing out of place there will be few surprises and no confusion to deal with. This attitude may carry over into food preferences as well as eating style, with compulsive individuals preferring simple straightforward foods rather than complex mixtures or casseroles.

In summary, then, it may be said that long-term preferences for specific foods seem to be acquired, although there are innate physiological bases for some preferences. Within a given culture or among persons with similar backgrounds there is considerable agreement as to what is most and least liked, although there are also large individual differences. Many of the most important variables contributing to preferences for particular foods fall under the general headings of familiarity or exposure, moderate novelty, and the tendency to imitate the preferences and eating habits of those around us, especially those who are respected or admired. Personality traits or characteristics probably have some effect on food preferences.

Long-term preferences are relatively stable, once established, and show little change from year to year. There seem to be somewhat different bases for liking and disliking. Disliked foods are always disliked, but the desire for preferred foods may fluctuate widely from day to day and even within a given day. Some of the reasons for these fluctuations are discussed in the following chapter.

CHAPTER 3

Fluctuations in Food Preferences

One of the first principles of food preferences is that disliked foods are always disliked regardless of the circumstances under which they are served. On the other hand, preferences for liked foods vary with conditions. Even those foods of which we are ordinarily very fond are not always liked or preferred. Under certain circumstances we find them highly unappealing and refuse to eat them. At other times, they are simply neutral and can be taken or left alone. Fluctuation and not stability is the rule rather than the exception in food preferences.

What accounts for fluctuations in food preferences, so that what we want today we didn't want yesterday but may want again tomorrow? There are many possible reasons. Some have to do with changes within the individual, while others have to do with the characteristics of the foods or the conditions or circumstances under which they are served. Research has been concentrated on long-term preferences, thus relatively little is known about daily fluctuations. This is due partly to the confusion between preferences and selections. In most of our daily lives we eat foods not because of some strong preference for them but simply because they are there.

Context

We find rich brown gravy delicious over mashed potatoes, but it would be repulsive over ice cream. Nor would we like orange soufflé as a side dish for spaghetti and meatballs. Preferences are affected by the broad context or setting in which the food appears.

The way in which an object is perceived and even its meaning are determined, in part, by its *context*. Context refers to the setting in which a particular stimulus occurs. It is all the other stimuli present with the given object or stimulus. The context can be simple, consisting only of other lines as in the illusions shown above, or it can be complex and include the whole

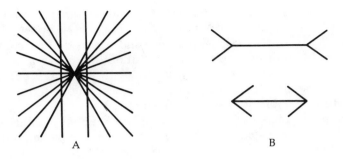

3–1. Hering (A) and Muller-Lyer (B) illusions

physical and social setting. In perception, classic examples are the Hering and Muller-Lyer illusions shown in figure 3-1. In the Hering illusion, the vertical lines are straight and parallel, but they appear to bow outward because of the context of radiating lines. In the Muller-Lyer illusion, the horizontal lines are the same length, but they appear to be different because of the context of arrow heads and tails in which they occur.

Context can alter not only the physical appearance of stimuli but also their meaning. The role of context in the perception of personality traits was discussed earlier in connection with the familiarity-preference hypothesis. In social perception, a risqué story told at a party is amusing, but the same story told at a loved one's funeral becomes gross and indecent, as does the person who tells it.

Food Contexts

The contexts for any item in a meal are all the other foods or food components present, the way in which the food is served, and all those other things that have to do with the actual service and setting. The ideas, thoughts, and feelings present with a particular food are also part of the context, and, like the radiating lines in the Hering illusion, they can alter the meaning and seeming taste of that food.

Method of serving: Different contexts are sometimes simply the different ways in which foods are prepared or served. Boiled or steamed rice served with butter and salt and pepper is a substitute for potatoes. The same rice, identical in flavor and texture, served with cream and syrup or whipped cream and fruit becomes a dessert. Even though the rice is the same, our perception of it is different because it is served in a different way. Crêpes filled with jelly and sprinkled with powdered sugar do not seem to be the same as crêpes filled with crabmeat and served with Mornay sauce. Fried and baked apples both have the sweet-sourness of apple, but one is served as a vegetable and the other as a dessert. Cheese and crackers served before a meal are an appetizer; after a meal they become an extra course.

Other foods: Pleasant colors or sounds become jarring and unpleasant in juxtaposition with some colors and sounds, but they go pleasantly with others. Similarly, some foods go together and others do not: corned beef and cabbage, frankfurters and beans, pie (but not cream pie) and ice cream are favorite combinations; apple sauce goes with roast pork but not with fried liver. Sometimes there is a natural fittingness among foods, based on flavor, texture, or appearance, so that one food complements the other. Complementarity is one of the goals of menu planning. A light vegetable goes well with fillet of sole, but a heavy one does not. At other times, there may be a physiological basis for the pairings in that one food aids the assimilation of nutrients from the other. There is a synergistic relation between baked beans and Boston brown bread, so that eating one helps in the digestion of the other. Finally, some foods seem to go together because they have been served together in the past for reasons of economy, practicality, preference, or culture. Once we become accustomed to particular combinations, they seem natural and correct. Americans put catsup on french fries, but Canadians sprinkle them with vinegar. (The acid in both may help to cut the grease.)

Whenever food is taken out of its usual context or presented in a different context, its meaning may be changed and the preference altered. (Occasionally the meaning doesn't change. Yorkshire pudding is almost identical with Dutch pancakes. One who is familiar with Dutch pancakes but not with Yorkshire pudding might ask for jelly for the pudding, to the consternation of the host or hostess.)

Changes in customary food pairings also are unpleasant. Bacon and eggs, chicken and dumplings, peaches and cream, or coffee and doughnuts are traditional pairings, and, even if available, few people would order coffee and dumplings, eggs and cream, or chicken and peaches. However, chicken can be prepared with peaches, and eggs can be poached in cream or have a bit of cream poured over them, and persons with initial negative reactions might find the dishes delicious if they tried them. Sometimes combinations that seem uninviting at first are quite appetizing and even commonly practiced in slightly altered forms. Sugar on meat or fish sounds bizarre, but it is used in curing both. A sprinkling of sugar enhances the flavor of bacon; sweet raisin or pineapple sauce is served with ham; no one objects to pancake syrup sloshing onto sausages; and sweet-sour sauces go with meat, vegetables, and desserts.

Order of presentation: The order in which foods are served affects food preferences. A hot roast beef sandwich offered after a caramel sundae would not have the same appeal as one offered before; nor would vegetables be appealing after dessert. During meals, foods usually are served in a specific order or sequence (Douglas 1979). In many cultures, there is a heavy main course of meat, fish, or poultry followed by a lighter, sweet one for dessert. In a typical British or North American meal, the main course is usually hot, and potatoes and vegetables accompany the meat; dessert is sweet and usually cold. Tea or coffee finishes the meal.

In some cultures, meals do not center around a heavy main course. Practices also differ within geographical settings. Farm families often have as hearty a meal at noon as in the evening. Among city dwellers, the main Sunday meal may be in the evening as it is on other days of the week, or it may be a dinner in early afternoon with a light lunch at night.

Social and economic changes in a society affect the way foods are served. At full-course dinners forty or fifty years ago, salad usually was served after the main meat course as a break between the main dish and the dessert. This is still done in many countries and sometimes at formal dinners in the United States, but more often salad starts the meal. Probably this change came about as a result of increased eating out before the widespread use of frozen and preprepared foods in restaurants. Serving the salad first gave the chef time to prepare the main dish. Although that time is no longer needed, the custom remains.

Why the traditional practice has been abandoned in private homes is somewhat perplexing. With the absence of cooks and maids, the host or hostess could join the guests and begin the meal by serving the main dish when it was ready rather than trying to keep it hot during a salad course. After the main dish, the guests could enjoy the salad while dessert was being readied for serving. The traditional sequence may be better digestively as well, but common sense does not always prevail over custom, once the custom is established.

Setting and time: Time and place are also contexts that affect food preferences. Some foods are for meals; others are for snacks. Some are served within the family; others are for formal entertainment. There are breakfast, lunch, and dinner foods. No one wants sandwiches for breakfast even though the components that make up a favorite sandwich are eaten then: toast, bacon, eggs; or bread, butter, jelly. The Florida citrus growers have spent thousands of dollars trying to convince us that "orange juice isn't just for breakfast anymore." Hearty breakfasts are nutritious, but few people take the time to prepare them and many wouldn't feel like eating them; thus, simple, easily prepared foods have become standard at breakfast and have come to seem inappropriate in other time contexts.

The social setting or context is also important. We enjoy food and tend to eat more when we are with other people (Klesges et al. 1983; Krantz 1979). The effect is most pronounced in a friendly atmosphere when the group is small, and it may also depend on the food (Berry et al. 1985). Some reports suggest that people want to eat more when they are alone or lonely, but the preference for food is generally higher during positive emotions such as friendliness, happiness, and joy (Lyman 1982a, 1982b). Elderly persons who live alone and are socially isolated show less interest in food and eating (Rao 1975; Sherwood 1973; Tempro 1978).

The physical setting in which food is served also affects food preferences. We like hotdogs at a picnic or a ballgame but not at a formal wedding reception. A humdrum meal in a friendly setting with a convivial crowd can become an exciting occasion. An intimate atmosphere with one we love can make mediocre food a nostalgic memory.

Lighting and decor: Bright lights make people more active. Soft lights are conducive to relaxation and slower movements (Birren 1969). In bright illumination people want foods that can be eaten quickly, whereas with soft, low lighting, they prefer to take time eating. Restaurant designers take advantage of this. In fast-food establishments where the profit on each item is small and depends on quick turnover, bright lights and starker furnishings are used. A quieter atmosphere with soft illumination can be used to advantage where the margin of profit is greater and a quick turnover is not required.

The color of the light is also important (Birren 1969). Red light increases activity and tension, people feel warmer, and time seems to pass faster. Green and blue lights have opposite effects, somewhat similar to those of dimmer illumination. People look best in warm illumination as given off by ordinary incandescent lamps. Warm fluorescent light also has a pleasing effect, but the fixtures are not attractive in the home, and some people are sensitive to the flicker of fluorescent lighting. Warm colors create a friendlier atmosphere than cool colors do, and make a room look smaller and more intimate.

Restaurant decor is designed to create an atmosphere that enhances the pleasantness of foods, sometimes by using light and color and other times by evoking appropriate associations—a country inn for family dinners or an English pub for fish and chips. Of course, there are limitations to what physical settings can accomplish. They cannot turn bad food into a gourmet's delight, but fresh flowers, sparkling crystal, gleaming silver, shining china, and crisp linens can certainly make us think the food is better than it is. Bad settings have the reverse effect. Liked foods become less preferred, and can even become revolting if we are in a smelly restaurant with dirty linen and sloppy service. A truly unpleasant experience may change the preferences permanently.

Associations as contexts: In addition to changing the meanings of foods, physical and social settings can arouse desires or preferences for particular foods because of associations from the past. The sight of foods or the odors and sounds associated with them create specific desires and preferences. When we smell baking bread, hear a sizzling steak, or pass an ice cream shop, we may suddenly have a craving for the foods although we were not hungry before and the thought of eating one of them had not crossed our minds.

Similarly, the presence or even the thought of objects, situations, or people associated with eating specific foods can create a desire for them.

We want popcorn at movies and cotton candy at carnivals, and a picnic is not a picnic without potato salad. As evening approaches, we begin to think of dinner foods even though hunger could be satisfied as well by lunch or breakfast items. If we wake up hungry in the morning, we never crave roast beef or baked lasagna.

These associations may play a dominant role in arousing desires for specific foods. Certainly, the number of connections is enormous, but we are not consciously aware of most of them. Since we recognize the desire but not the conditions initiating it, we think the desire has arisen spontaneously. In fact, it might be due to the presence of conditioned stimuli whose association with the desire we do not recognize or to the presence of stimuli we simply have not noticed. We are not consciously aware of many of the stimuli to which we make responses, and the response of desiring a particular food should be no exception.

The Effect of Eating on Food Selections and Preferences

Hunger seems an obvious reason for fluctuations in preferences, but that explanation is too simplistic. Not only do we eat when we are not hungry, but we also refuse some foods when we are hungry. Hunger alone cannot account for eating or not eating, and it cannot fully account for fluctuations in our likings for specific foods, although it does play a role.

Satiation and Pleasantness

Eating changes the pleasantness ratings of foods. In some cases, sweet substances and food-related smells (but not nonfood smells) that were rated pleasant when individuals were hungry were rated unpleasant after they had eaten (Duclaux et al. 1973). The smells need not be related to the food just eaten. For example, an orange smell as well as the sweetness of sucrose become unpleasant after one has taken glucose or sucrose (Cabanac 1971). In additional studies using actual foods rather than odors, it was found that the rated pleasantness of foods just eaten decreased while that for other foods was relatively unchanged, showing only slight decreases or, in a few cases, slight increases (Rolls et al. 1981). Thus, both a change in hunger and our having eaten a food can temporarily change our liking for it.

After we eat a food its taste becomes less pleasant to us and we want less of it. Some foods have a greater satiating effect than others. Tomato soup as an appetizer reduces caloric intake in a meal more than do appetizers of crackers, jelly, and juice (Kissileff et al. 1984). Solid foods seem more filling than liquids, and so do foods that need to be chewed. In controlled laboratory studies, eating a specific food decreases the amount of that food eaten later, but if given a different food in the second course, individuals will eat almost as much as they did in the first course (Rolls et al. 1980). This is not uncommon among lower animals, who will stop eating one food but will start eating another if it is presented. Humans seem to behave the same way. Some lower animals even start eating the same food again if the remainder is taken away after they have stopped eating and it is then presented again.

Sensory-specific satiety: The decrease in the desire for a specific food after eating it is known as *sensory-specific satiety* because it is most common for foods with the same sensory characteristics. The reason for the changes is unclear. In some studies the second rating of the food's pleasantness was made two minutes after eating. This does not allow time for the food to be absorbed, so the decreased pleasantness was not due to a change in nutrient needs or a biological reduction in hunger. In other studies, time lapses that allowed for partial absorption and digestion were used.

In all studies the time between eating and the second pleasantness rating was usually less than an hour, but everyday experience suggests the effect can last for hours or days, not because of changes in hunger or nutritional needs but because of our interest in variety and change. It is simply boring to have the same main dish, vegetables, sandwiches, or desserts two or more days in a row (Rolls et al., Variety in a meal, 1981). Oddly, however, boredom and the need for variety are selective. They have little effect on breakfast choices; we usually have potatoes and bread or rolls at every dinner; and we drink the same beverages several times a day. Perhaps these constancies give some needed continuity to our lives. Or, repetition may give us reassurance. Repetitive behavior often occurs when one is under pressure, and perhaps breakfast, especially during the week, is one of those occasions when stress is present, even if it is nothing more than the stress of mobilizing the body to start a new day. On weekends, when the pressure of time is less, we tend to want more variety in our breakfasts, and we have more time to prepare them.

Variety in a meal is aesthetically pleasing, but it also increases the amount of food eaten (Rolls et al., Variety in a meal, 1981). Overeating on Thanksgiving and other holidays may be due more to the variety of foods offered than to custom. If we are filled with one food, we usually don't refuse a different one, and no matter how stuffed we are, we always seem to have room for dessert.

Self-Selection of Diets and the Wisdom of the Body

Are there innate physiological mechanisms that regulate food preferences and intakes? The possibility has intrigued psychologists and physiologists for years. There are homeostatic mechanisms that work much like a thermostat to regulate body temperature, sleep, and hunger. In rats, there seems to be such a mechanism governing the intake of some substances such as salt (Bartoshuk 1981). In humans the data are unclear, although the preference or intolerance for milk seems to be based on the body's ability to digest lactose (Kretchmer 1978), and recent studies suggest that an abundance of proteins or carbohydrates at breakfast may be compensated for at lunch (Wurtman and Wurtman 1984). Whether specific or even general classes of foods are self-selected with any regularity is still controversial, in spite of many years of research.

Self-Selection of Diets

Many years ago, it was discovered that, if left to make their own choices, newly weaned children eight to ten months old would select balanced, healthy diets. They might eat only one food for several days running and then switch to something else, but in the long run a proper diet was obtained (Davis 1928). Later studies with rats gave similar results (Richter 1942). Although the results are now thought to be due to learning, the findings became the basis for a popular belief that children would be nutritionally healthy if allowed to eat what they wanted. This was a great boon to parents. No longer did they need to worry about what their children ate. In fact, some were led to believe that the less they meddled with their children's eating habits, the healthier their children would be.

Unfortunately, there were several important considerations that the popularizers ignored. First, there were only three children in the study, which is much too small a sample to justify placing great confidence in the results. Second, the children were living in a hospital for the six months to a year covered by the study and were offered the foods by nurses. The hospital setting and professional care may have resulted in special treatment ensuring good health. Third, all the foods made available to the children were nutritionally healthy ones. The two possibilities open to the children were to choose balanced or unbalanced diets, not healthy or unhealthy ones. The study gave no indication of the kinds of foods children would select if they could choose freely from among both healthy and unhealthy foods.

Even if the self-selection results were correct under the very special limited conditions studied, they cannot be applied to individuals who do not meet those conditions. Given the opportunity, children eat poisons, colored crayons, ants, oranges, bread, and all kinds of healthy and unhealthy foods and nonfoods. Older children and adults consume untold amounts of candy bars, french fries, and soda pop—items that have little or no nutritional value or are unhealthy because they are chosen in preference to healthy foods.

In the real world, the self-selection of healthy diets based on the assumption of a preference for healthy foods must take into consideration the effects of curiosity, novelty, peer pressure, television commercials, and other onslaughts on human suggestibility. Even if our bodies once knew what was best for us and tended toward a balanced and healthy diet, it is unlikely they would freely do so now, at least not without appropriate exposure to healthful foods and some guidance in selecting them.

The Wisdom of the Body

Long before the studies on self-selection of diet, Walter Cannon, a physiologist, showed that the physiological changes that take place in hunger and strong emotions are those that help the individual cope with threat and stress (Cannon 1939). For example, during intense emotions, there is an increase in blood sugar, and breathing becomes deeper and more rapid in order to supply more oxygen to the blood and muscles. These and other changes enable us to carry out actions requiring greater vigor or strength than we have under normal circumstances; we can run faster, fight harder, lift more, and so on. There are other changes too. For example, there is less circulation of the blood near the surface of the skin. Thus, if one is cut there is less likelihood of severe bleeding. There is also less sensitivity to pain or, at least, a lessened awareness of pain.

Cannon hypothesized that emotions have an "emergency function" which helps the body prepare for or cope with dangerous and threatening situations. He was so impressed with the beneficial effects of those physiological changes as well as with the changes during hunger that he spoke of the "wisdom of the body" to emphasize the idea that the body, if left to its own devices, would do what was best to cope with existing conditions. Unfortunately, the wisdom of the body, unlike that of Solomon, is at times shortsighted. In intense emotions, the hand shakes and trembles, and if safety in the situation requires the precise and delicate finger movements needed for tying off an artery, injecting a serum, or removing a splinter from the eye, the "emergency function" makes these acts impossible.

In spite of reservations regarding the wisdom of the body and the efficiency of the self-selection of diets, the studies do show that there is a tendency for the body to cope with disequilibrium and adverse situations and to restore the body to an optimal level of physiological functioning. Although these tendencies may be too vague to produce specific food preferences, they may dispose individuals to preferences for general classes of foods, and these preferences may be made more precise by exposure, past experience, and other conditions operating at the time.

Emotions and Moods

Although the variables and conditions discussed above are related to fluctuations in food preferences, desires for specific foods seem to change more often than can be explained readily by most of them. Many changes occur in a single day without there being a comparable number of changes in contexts or physiological states to account for the preference shifts.

What is needed to explain the shifts is some variable that changes a number of times a day and has a physiological and psychological basis. The conditioned stimuli discussed above may have that function. Research by the author suggests that feelings and emotions also may play such a role. That research and the food-mood relation are discussed in the following chapter.

CHAPTER 4

The Relation Between Emotions and Food Preferences

Individuals in the burgeoning field of psychonutrition and psycho-dietetics have argued that foods determine our moods—"We are what we eat" (Cheraskin et al. 1976; Watson 1972). This point of view is best known with respect to megavitamin therapy in the treatment of schizophrenia (Pauling and Hawkins 1980) and the effects of sugar in causing depression (Dufty 1975). The view itself is widely held by some herbalists and adherents of folk medicine and goes back to Greek times, but it is difficult to find well-controlled scientific studies supporting the assertion.

Another widespread belief is that just as foods determine our moods so do our moods determine what we eat. The view is part of our folklore, but when one tries to find out just what foods are preferred during different emotions there are few specific answers. Many are quite general, suggesting, for example, that individuals tend to drink milk when sad, eat a great deal when bored, or eat high-calorie desserts when frustrated (Gifft et al. 1976).

If there is a relation between emotions and food preferences, it may better account for those fluctuations in preferences that often occur outside any food contexts or are too far removed in time from previous eating for sensory-specific satiety to be effective. Even when fluctuations are due to the presence of unrecognized conditioned stimuli, as suggested in the preceding chapter, emotions may act as the bridge between the stimulus and the desire for specific foods.

Current Research

Several studies by the author have sought to determine the relation between specific emotions and food preferences.

44

Emotions and Preferred Food Items

In one study, 100 college or university students—20 in a commercial food-preparation course, 50 in an evening introductory psychology course, and 30 in a regular advanced psychology course—were asked to imagine themselves clearly experiencing 22 different emotions and to indicate what foods they would like to eat or drink during each (Lyman 1982a). The results are shown in tables 4-1 and 4-2.

In table 4-1, reading down a column, shows how often different menu items were preferred during a given emotion; reading across a row shows how often a given menu item was preferred during different emotions. Where applicable, the largest row percents are marked in italics to show when each food item was most preferred. Table 4-2 shows how much different menu categories contributed to the overall food preferences.

The results clearly show that different food preferences are associated with different emotions. The high percentage of "anything" responses during boredom suggests that preferences are least specific during that emotion. Interestingly, the largest preference for desserts, which are usually sweet, was during joy and not depression as is commonly believed. Also, the largest preference for alcohol was not during anger, frustration, or depression when it is supposedly used to alleviate the feelings, but during love-affection, when individuals reported using wine with meals to prolong the mood.

Emotions and Nutritional Values of Preferred Foods

In a second study, the same procedure was used with 100 university students in a lower-level psychology course, but the data were analyzed for the nutritional values and the traditional food-group characteristics of the foods preferred during the various emotions (Lyman 1982b). The nutritional values were determined by using Jacobson's *Nutrition Scoreboard* (Jacobson 1975), with values of minus 10 or less as junk foods, plus 10 or more as healthful foods, and minus 9 to plus 9 as half-and-half foods. The results are shown in table 4-3.

Statistical treatment, using Cochran's Q Test (Daniel 1978), showed that, except for alcohol, the differences among emotions were all significant. Different preferences clearly go with different emotions. An examination of the table shows that healthful foods were most preferred during positive emotions, and junk foods were more likely to be preferred during negative emotions.

Emotions and Preferred Food Textures

For a random half of the students, a subsequent analysis of the data was made to identify the textural and physical characteristics ("mouthfeel") of

Food Preferences

TABLE **4-1.** **Percentage of individuals stating preferences for each food item during different emotions**[1]

Food	Amused	Angry	Anxious	Bored	Depressed	Embarrassed	Excited	Fearful	Friendly	Frustrated	Guilty
Salad	5	1	2	2	-	5	6	1	5	2	-
Soup	2	4	6	5	2	3	2	4	-	2	1
Eggs	3	-	3	3	-	1	2	2	3	1	1
Fish	2	2	-	1	1	-	1	1	1	2	2
Meat	7	9	11	11	8	4	9	2	22	8	9
Poultry	3	2	-	-	-	-	1	1	-	-	-
Casseroles	-	2	2	5	2	3	1	-	7	2	2
Fast foods	11	3	6	2	2	2	3	1	17	3	2
Vegetables	9	8	3	1	4	2	12	2	20	7	6
Cheese	7	1	1	3	3	-	5	1	5	2	1
Fruit	7	8	6	4	4	3	6	1	9	10	4
Sandwich	2	8	8	6	3	1	3	4	3	5	4
Dessert	15	3	3	12	3	8	9	1	9	5	6
Milk	-	-	5	1	3	1	3	1	1	2	1
Juice	-	-	2	3	-	-	1	-	-	1	-
Snack, healthy	14	5	20	28	13	6	13	7	10	14	6
Snack, junk	27	12	22	25	12	9	13	11	5	15	11
Beverage, nonalcoholic	5	6	11	5	15	6	9	14	7	6	7
Alcohol	4	8	-	-	6	1	2	1	6	6	2
Nothing[2]	9	36	19	7	23	37	27	45	5	18	33
Anything[3]	4	3	4	19	11	2	2	1	12	4	1
Not sure[2]	8	5	2	1	-	16	4	5	3	5	7

[1]Based on the number of respondents who said they preferred a specific food.
[2]Based on the total number of respondents (N = 100).
[3]Based on the number of respondents who said they preferred some food.

Reprinted by permission from: Lyman, B. (1982). Menu item preferences and emotions, *School Food Service Research Review*, 6(1): 32–35.

TABLE 4-1. Percentage of individuals stating preferences for each food item during different emotions[1] (continued)

Food	Happy	Hostile	Jealous	Joy	Lonely	Love	Relaxed	Sad	Self-confident	Solemn	Worried	Average
Salad	5	-	3	5	2	*12*	5	2	11	6	2	4
Soup	1	2	1	1	*8*	-	1	*8*	2	6	2	3
Eggs	1	-	2	2	2	2	3	-	3	1	1	2
Fish	4	-	-	8	1	4	5	1	*15*	3	1	2
Meat	*29*	10	7	19	9	28	15	5	26	23	2	12
Poultry	3	3	-	1	-	1	3	-	6	5	1	1
Casseroles	6	1	-	5	4	2	2	1	*8*	3	2	3
Fast foods	12	2	3	8	7	6	7	2	4	2	1	5
Vegetables	23	5	8	18	9	16	16	3	11	18	11	10
Cheese	6	-	1	-	5	4	4	-	6	2	-	3
Fruit	*11*	5	5	5	4	10	10	7	7	7	5	6
Sandwich	4	-	5	1	9	2	2	4	3	3	7	4
Dessert	15	3	7	*19*	8	10	8	3	1	3	2	7
Milk	2	1	-	1	2	1	2	1	-	2	2	1
Juice	1	-	2	-	-	-	1	-	1	-	2	1
Snack, healthy	13	10	9	2	17	9	12	8	7	8	14	11
Snack, junk	9	10	6	9	16	7	5	7	1	3	18	12
Beverage, nonalcoholic	6	3	7	3	13	3	22	20	6	8	17	9
Alcohol	6	-	3	7	5	*14*	10	2	3	-	1	4
Nothing[2]	3	41	28	11	13	18	5	36	7	17	30	21
Anything[3]	8	2	3	12	5	12	10	3	14	5	2	6
Not sure[2]	3	12	14	3	5	6	3	4	3	9	1	5

TABLE 4-2. Percentage of total food preferences contributed by items in each menu category[1]

Category	Amused	Angry	Anxious	Bored	Depressed	Embarrassed	Excited	Fearful	Friendly	Frustrated
	Emotion									
	%									
Soup/salad	6	5	6	6	3	11	8	8	3	5
Entree (main dish)	7	16	11	10	10	10	14	6	19	9
Vegetables	6	10	3	-	4	4	9	3	13	6
Dessert	12	4	3	12	2	15	8	3	8	6
Beverage, nonalcoholic	3	9	18	9	24	16	15	25	5	10
Snacks	39	20	40	52	33	30	25	36	13	33

[1]Column sums do not equal 100 percent because preferences for eggs, fast foods, sandwiches, and alcohol were not included in the menu categories unless clearly appropriate.

Reprinted by permission from: Lyman, B. (1982). Menu item preferences and emotions. *School Food Service Research Review*, 6(1): 32–35.

foods preferred during different emotions. The characteristics used were: warm, chilled, unheated, crunchy, soft, liquid, solid, sweet, spicy, sour, and salty. The results are shown in table 4-4. They indicate that the frequency with which different characteristics are preferred varies widely with emotions. Cochran's Test showed significant differences among emotions for all characteristics except spicy and sour.

Emotions and Foods Preferred and Eaten

In a third study, the procedure in Study 2 was used with 29 university students in an advanced psychology course on feelings and emotions. In addition, they were asked to keep a record of what they actually ate while experiencing those emotions. The same analyses were carried out except that junk food was more broadly defined to include those half-and-half and healthful foods on which, as snack items, individuals might fill up at the expense of a more balanced intake. Also, the data were tallied to include full meals as well as individual food items.

Food preferences: Several findings are of particular interest. First, healthful foods were preferred significantly more often than junk foods only during excitement, self-confidence, and solemnness, and junk foods were pre-

TABLE 4-2. **Percentage of total food preferences contributed by items in each menu category[1] (continued)**

Category	Emotion												
	Guilty	Happy	Hostile	Jealous	Joy	Lonely	Love	Relaxed	Sad	Self-confident	Solemn	Worried	Average
	%												
Soup/salad	3	3	4	4	4	10	6	2	13	10	11	4	6
Entree (main dish)	18	31	31	11	25	9	24	24	9	48	29	7	17
Vegetables	9	13	9	9	13	9	11	11	4	7	17	10	8
Dessert	9	10	5	9	20	4	6	6	4	-	4	3	7
Beverage, nonalcoholic	13	6	11	14	4	14	4	23	28	6	11	26	13
Snacks	24	14	28	24	12	29	14	15	18	7	12	33	25

ferred significantly more often during amusement. This contrasts with significantly greater preferences for healthful foods in 14 of the emotions when "healthful" includes items that are nutritionally sound but that, nevertheless, are likely to interfere with a balanced diet (table 4-3).

Correlation between foods preferred and eaten: Second, the correlations between the nutritional values of preferred and eaten foods were significant for only six of the 22 emotions. These were anger, depression, guilt, jealousy, self-confidence, and solemnness. The correlation for solemnness was negative. There was clearly no relation between the nutritional values of preferred and eaten foods for amused, embarrassed, frustrated, happy, and joy. The discrepancy between foods preferred and those actually eaten showed up frequently and is to be expected. Selection depends on availability, and the reasons given for the discrepancies are familiar to most people: "I couldn't afford it," "It wasn't in the house," "I didn't want to take the time to fix it." This confirms the suspicion that food items in the home may be there more because of advertising and affordability than because of carefully considered preferences.

Emotions precede choices: Third, sweet foods and cereals and grains that may convert to sugars were eaten most often during depression. Junk foods, which are usually high in sugars, were eaten most often during depression, amusement, and friendliness. Study 2 showed that in general they were preferred more often during negative emotions. These findings

TABLE 4-3. **Frequency with which foods of various nutritional values and food group characteristics were preferred during different emotions (N = 100)**

Emotion	Nutritional value[1]				Food group[2]					
	H	J	½	N	DP	ME	FV	CG	AL	OT
Amusement	31*	17	31	9	20	23	42	32	4	24
Anger	29*	11	21	36	3	19	18	19	8	26
Anxiety	33*	16	28	18	8	23	21	22	0	42
Boredom	23	21	48	4	15	16	29	31	0	52
Depression	29	17	30	21	13	14	13	22	9	36
Embarrassment	23	12	11	31	7	10	13	6	1	22
Excitement	37*	8	23	24	15	14	24	16	0	30
Fear	21	12	16	41	6	4	10	12	1	26
Friendliness	53*	9	31	4	25	30	40	38	6	27
Frustration	33*	18	24	17	7	16	25	23	5	28
Guilt	28	17	9	28	6	14	18	13	2	22
Happiness	53*	11	32	3	23	43	43	34	6	24
Hostility	23*	6	13	35	4	18	10	11	0	15
Jealousy	25	13	13	24	5	11	16	13	3	20
Joy	36	23	22	9	12	28	25	23	7	29
Loneliness	33*	15	28	12	15	21	27	30	3	35
Love	35*	6	30	14	16	29	30	22	13	20
Relaxation	39*	6	38	7	16	28	31	18	5	42
Sadness	26*	8	24	31	3	8	18	15	2	30
Self-confidence	62*	1	22	7	13	42	27	20	3	23
Solemnness	46*	3	17	16	5	27	24	12	0	21
Worry	25	16	23	28	10	13	21	19	2	33

Note: Q's: H = 130.98; J = 69.70; ½ = 104.33; N = 223.19; DP = 95.49; ME = 150.32; FV = 75.78; CG = 99.56; AL = 10.29; OT = 85.36; all p's = .001 except AL = .98.

[1] H = Healthful; J = junk; ½ = half-and-half; N = nothing (see text for further explanation).

[2] DP = dairy products; ME = meats and eggs; FV = fruits and vegetables; CG = cereals and grains; AL = alcohol; OT = all other items.

* Preference for healthful foods was significantly greater than for junk foods (chi square) at the .05 or better level.

Reprinted by permission from: Lyman, B. (1982). The nutritional values and food group characteristics of foods preferred during various emotions. *Journal of Psychology*, 112: 121–27. Reprinted with permission of the Helen Dwight Reid Educational Foundation. Published by Heldref Publications, 4000 Albemarle St., N.W., Washington, D.C. 20016. Copyright © 1982.

suggest that the psychonutritionists may be confusing cause and effect—in some instances, at least. The argument is made that sugar, although it gives a temporary lift, causes depression in the long run, and that individuals become depressed as a result of high carbohydrate intakes. The studies here show that individuals were depressed *before* they ate sugars or sugar-laden foods. Is it, then, a fact that sugar causes depression? Or do depressed people simply eat more carbohydrates? Or is there some circular relation in which depression leads to eating carbohydrates which in turn

TABLE 4-4. **Percent of individuals preferring foods with the specified characteristics, during various emotions**

Emotion	Characteristics										
	Wm	Cl	Uh	Cr	Sf	Ld	Sd	Sw	Sp	Sr	St
Afraid	36	6	50	18	30	33	27	33	3	-	12
Amused	47	24	51	26	55	12	35	47	14	-	16
Angry	31	12	57	33	33	24	53	41	7	2	7
Anxious	40	14	56	28	37	33	28	33	-	2	33
Bored	27	17	60	38	35	17	27	35	-	-	29
Depressed	33	20	37	15	33	37	17	35	2	2	4
Embarrassed	29	16	40	13	37	26	18	29	5	-	5
Excited	40	25	40	28	45	20	30	30	5	3	12
Friendly	63	22	29	18	45	16	47	24	16	-	6
Frustrated	22	13	49	29	38	20	24	33	7	-	16
Guilty	50	11	28	8	45	22	20	31	3	-	6
Happy	64	26	40	20	66	20	52	44	14	2	10
Hostile	52	-	29	16	16	13	49	33	3	-	13
Jealous	20	22	50	20	45	25	17	25	-	3	8
Joyous	46	17	9	9	50	13	30	30	15	-	2
Lonely	54	19	26	26	44	33	28	33	12	-	19
Love	48	20	28	11	61	28	37	30	11	4	2
Relaxed	70	17	26	9	11	35	26	37	13	-	4
Sad	56	6	31	17	34	48	20	28	3	6	6
Self-confident	71	7	32	7	61	22	44	20	-	-	-
Solemn	73	4	25	6	52	10	44	10	12	-	2
Worried	34	13	58	26	40	26	18	42	-	-	8

Wm = warm; Cl = chilled; Uh = unheated; Cr = crunchy; Sf = soft; Ld = liquid; Sd = solid; Sw = sweet; Sp = spicy; Sr = sour; St = salty.

enhances depression? It is likely that the relation is a complex one. Certainly, one's choice of foods is not unaffected by moods and feelings.

General Conclusions

The results of the studies do not mean that there is a specific food preference for every conceivable emotion or that all individuals prefer the same foods during the same emotions. There are variations and individual differences, and somewhat different results might be found with other age groups or among individuals with different backgrounds. Nevertheless, there are trends and tendencies that clearly show a variety of complex relations between emotions and food preferences.

The studies as a whole suggest that individuals tend to prefer, but not always eat, what is best for them physiologically or psychologically. There seems to be some general "wisdom of the body" which may be as much the result of learning and experience as of some innate natural tendency. Food was least preferred during negative emotions when it would be difficult to digest and was most preferred when physiological conditions (feelings of happiness, self-confidence, and the like) were best for digestion. Full meals also were preferred most often during positive emotions. As noted above, junk foods, normally high in sugar, were preferred more often during negative emotions when a temporary lift might be desirable. During anger and fear (the emotions studied by Cannon), the ratio of individuals eating healthful as opposed to junk foods was two to one. Since those emotions involve fairly high energy expenditures, this suggests the body may be selecting foods to restore spent nutrients.

Psychological use of foods: Foods also tended to be used psychologically, to reduce or terminate undesirable emotions and to prolong pleasant or desirable ones. Crunchy foods were most often preferred when individuals were angry, bored, or frustrated, least preferred during self-confidence, and most often eaten during frustration. Individuals reported they wanted these to help reduce frustration or alleviate boredom. Apples were chosen during frustration because individuals wanted something they could bite into, and one person said she wanted an orange so she could rip off the skin. In boredom, variety was sought in foods, with the largest percent of "snack" responses occurring then (table 4-1). Soups, which carry an aura of hearth-and-home, were preferred most often when individuals were lonely or sad. In love, full meals with wine were used to prolong the experience, and the meals were likely to include gourmet dishes and lighter foods to fit the mood. Hearty "steak and potato" meals were chosen during self-confidence.

The Importance of Emotions in Food Preferences

How important are emotions in accounting for fluctuations in food preferences? At first glance, it might seem unlikely that they play any major role. After all, food preferences can change from hour to hour, and how many different emotions are experienced in a day or week? If it is only one or two, they cannot begin to be responsible for the variety of food preferences during the same period. Surprisingly, the number is much larger than expected. Many emotions are fleeting and very subtle. Many are also nameless. What is the name for the feeling at the sight of the year's first snow? Or at the smell of rain on a dusty field? Even before getting out of bed in the morning we may have gone through a series of named and nameless emotions: an uneasy feeling about the coming day or concern for an absent friend; the pleasant recollection of last night's supper or the thought of a phone call to be made. When one takes into consideration the subtle, weak, and fleeting emotions as well as the stronger, more lasting ones, the number per day can be surprisingly large. As reported by 60 university students in a recent survey by the author, the average number of *different* emotions experienced in a day was 31. The smallest number was 11, and the largest was 86. In the same survey, the students reported experiencing emotions 50 times a day, on average. The smallest number of times was 13 and the largest was 155. The actual numbers of different emotions and emotion experiences per day are probably much larger because the students reported difficulty in keeping accurate records. If food preferences and choices depend on emotions, the figures show that there are enough emotions occurring often enough to account for tremendous daily variability and fluctuation.

Reasons for the Emotion-Food Preference Relation

Why do the relations found in the studies exist? Why should there be fairly specific food preferences going with different emotions? The reasons are both physiological and psychological.

Physiological reasons: The different physiological changes in different emotions may contribute to food preferences. Different emotions show themselves in different ways—dryness in the throat, for example, or heaviness in the stomach—which clearly affect food preferences. Emotions also show themselves in many other much more subtle sensations which are experienced even though they are not easily measured with objective measuring devices (Lyman and Waters 1986). Such subtle sensations may go unnoticed unless direct attention is focused on them, but they may be strong enough, nevertheless, to influence food preferences at a nonconscious level. Fuller knowledge of the physiology of emotions and of nutrition, ingestion, and digestion is needed. It may help to clarify the role played by the "wisdom of the body" in food preferences and choices.

Some researchers report that there are different kinds of experienced hungers (Pearson and Pearson 1976)—for example, hunger in the mouth or hunger in the stomach. Unless the specific hunger is satisfied, individuals may continue to eat until by accident they happen upon the food that reduces the particular hunger. Certainly, most persons have had the experience of feeling vaguely hungry and eating one thing and then another only to remain unsated. It has been suggested that if overweight persons took the time to figure out what they really wanted to eat, and then ate it, weight problems would tend to diminish. Rather than continuing to nibble, they would eat only the one food they craved, and thus they would actually take in fewer calories even if the preferred food were high in calories. Specific hungers have not been tied to specific emotions, but it seems reasonable to expect relationships between specific hungers and specific emotions. By paying attention to sensory qualities, more appropriate fits could be made between the physical characteristics of foods and the physiological characteristics of emotions. This area of research still needs to be undertaken.

Psychological reasons: The associations between emotions and food preferences may have been acquired from experiences in the past when specific foods were eaten while the person was experiencing strong emotions or subtle feelings. For example, from early childhood, sweet desserts are served at parties and on other joyous occasions; fast foods often are eaten with other persons in a friendly atmosphere. These associations may carry over so that experiencing those feelings now influences preferences and choices. The fact that there are similarities among individuals in the foods preferred during emotions would depend on the similarity of backgrounds and cultural experiences. Differences in backgrounds would account for individual differences in preferences. This hypothesis needs to be tested cross-culturally to see if individuals with different backgrounds prefer different foods when experiencing the same emotions. In the meantime, the best tentative conclusion is that both physiology and psychology contribute to the relation between emotions and preferred foods.

Implications of the Research

If different food preferences are associated with different emotions and if different emotions evoke fairly specific food preferences, it is interesting to speculate whether eating those foods would evoke the feelings and emotions with which they are associated. For example, if fast foods are associated with feelings of friendliness, will eating fast foods put one in a friendly mood? Will salads make one feel more loving? Many people think a sweet dessert cheers them up; in the studies above, desserts were preferred most often during joy. On the other hand, soups were preferred when people were lonely or sad, and crunchy foods were eaten most often during frustration, apparently to weaken the moods. If those foods were eaten when an individual was neither sad nor frustrated, would he or she begin to feel that way because the foods and feelings were associated in the past; or would the feelings become more positive? Learning theory suggests the latter: the response last made in the presence of a stimulus is the one that becomes most strongly associated. Therefore, if eating the foods made one feel better in spite of negative feelings to begin with, they should make the person feel better now and should strengthen positive feelings. Similarly, foods that made a person feel worse or strengthened a negative emotion should have a negative effect later by creating or strengthening a negative mood or weakening a positive one.

The use of foods to modify feelings and emotions is being researched currently but has not yet been established. Some tentative proposals for its application are made in chapter 13.

CHAPTER 5

Fads, Fashions, and Food Preferences

The preceding chapters dealt with fluctuations in food preferences as they occur for the individual, but food preferences also develop and change within whole segments of the population. These fluctuations occur as fads or fashions, which are as common in food preferences as they are in clothing, cars, housing, interior decoration, leisure activities, child rearing practices, applications of psychotherapy, and the use of language. A list of food fashions would include everything from soups through desserts, whole classes of foods such as fish and salads, and individual items such as oatmeal and Ovaltine. Interest that started long ago in some foods remains high, while interest in others is as dead as yesteryear's automobile tail fins. Has anyone served leg of mutton lately?

What triggers a fashion or fad? What keeps it going, and what causes one fashion to subside or to be replaced by another? Considering the nature of fads and fashions should help answer these questions.

General Nature of Fads and Fashions

Fads and fashions are forms of collective behavior that do not depend on true group structure (Brown 1965). Group structure involves common motives conducive to interaction, the development of role and status hierarchies, and the development of norms and standards regulating the behavior of individuals that is of consequence to the group (Sherif and Sherif 1969). Fads and fashions are more likely to involve a diffuse crowd or aggregate of individuals lacking the cohesiveness of a primary group. Thus, conformity to a fad or fashion is more or less voluntarily sought and accepted by individuals rather than being imposed upon them. Of course, advertisements as well as parental, peer, and social pressures may activate or strengthen the desire to conform.

Distinction Between Fads and Fashions

Social psychologists have not been consistent in distinguishing between fads and fashions, and when distinctions are made, they are often unclear or confusing. However, there is some agreement on the following points.

Fashions and prestige: Fashions tend to be introduced by high-status individuals and have status or prestige value within society as a whole (Turner and Killian 1972). For this reason fashions create some social cohesiveness (Blumer 1968) in which the boundaries between classes are weakened because all are engaging in the same behavior. Although both fads and fashions tend to bring people together and give them a sense of belonging, and both can express differences in prestige (Smelser 1963), fads are more restricted in scope. They carry prestige value within a smaller group, and subscribing or not subscribing to them may or may not affect a person's general social status.

Fads as protests: Fads may involve a protest against the existing behavior or values of some group, but what starts out as a fad can become a fashion. In the 1960s, men wore long hair as a sign of protest; then long hair for men became fashionable. Vegetarianism shows a somewhat similar trend: what began as a fad (or perhaps a cult) years ago has now become almost fashionable.

Continuity of fashions and custom: Fads may arise spontaneously and capriciously (Turner and Killian 1972), but fashions tend to emerge from existing patterns of behavior. Fashions have a connection with custom. They have been defined as custom disguised as a departure from custom (Sapir 1969), and they may have a nostalgic quality harking back to an earlier time. Unlike fads, changes in fashions may result from changes in environmental needs, although this is not true of all fashions. Certainly it is difficult to see how environmental needs apply to changes in clothing fashions.

Duration of fads and fashions: Fads tend to be shorter lived than fashions (Miller 1985), and their appearance and disappearance are usually sudden. Fashions, on the other hand, tend to emerge more slowly, and their disappearance is characterized by changes in the fashion and a rather gradual transition to a new fashion.

The discussion above shows that fads and fashions are not clearly different from one another and that the differences are more a matter of degree than of kind. Fashions are the primary concern of the following discussion, but insofar as fads and fashions are similar, the points made apply to both.

The Growth and Decline of Fashions

Like novels and plays, fashions have a beginning, a middle, and an end. They also have rebirths, although each reoccurrence is somewhat different from the one before (Turner and Killian 1972). The long skirts of the mid-

1980s were not the same as those of the mid-1930s, and the Victorian-style houses of today are not replicas of earlier ones.

Fads as well as fashions go through a cycle of growth and decline (Brown 1965; Miller 1985). They begin with a latent period, which is characteristically a time of discovery when behavior or items commonly used by a limited number of individuals are discovered by persons outside that group. The hula hoop, for example, was used originally in physical education classes in Australia. Often the discovered item or behavior is commonplace. Before it became popular in the rest of North America, Cajun food had been known in southern Louisiana for generations. In other cases, such as clothing, automobiles, and even haute cuisine, designers may create the particular styles, and conscious efforts may be made to bring attention to the styles.

During the explosion, or peaking, period that follows the latent period, the behavior is adopted by individuals outside the original group, and the fad or fashion spreads. Then there is a widespread surge in adoption, sometimes at a feverish pace. Word of mouth, personal interaction, and especially the media foster the spread of interest. Massive advertising campaigns may be used to create the desire to copy or to imitate the behavior, or the fad or fashion may snowball on its own.

Ultimately a peak of satiation is reached. The fashion may become established custom and continue, or interest may begin to wane, in which case the fashion fades. During the period of decline, there is boredom with or indifference to the fashion, and negative feelings toward it may develop. Individuals who continue with the fashion are considered boors and clearly out-of-date. A new fashion may replace the old one, and the cycle of growth and decline is repeated.

Reasons for the Growth and Decline of Fashions

Boredom, novelty, and familiarity: The trilogy of boredom, novelty, and familiarity is one reason for the growth and decline of fashion. As discussed earlier, people often see familiar things as boring and dissatisfying, while new things evoke curiosity and interest. This leads to an eager acceptance of the different and unfamiliar (providing it is not too radically unfamiliar), and a new fad or fashion is underway. Interest peaks, the unfamiliar becomes familiar, disinterest sets in, and the fashion wanes. Another cycle begins with boredom setting the stage for our embracing a new fashion.

Psychological needs: Psychological needs make up another set of conditions conducive to fashion changes. Subscribing to a fad or fashion satisfies a need for acceptance and affiliation by giving a feeling of identity and unity with members of a group to which one aspires to belong (Miller 1985). Fashion also gives one a sense of self-importance. It satisfies a need for prestige (Sapir 1969) and is used to assert a distinctiveness from others

(Smelser 1963). It communicates one's status and prestige (Miller 1985) and sets one apart from others by indicating the group or groups to which one does and does not belong. Individuals may abandon a fashion when it becomes so widespread that it no longer distinguishes them from others (Smelser 1963). For many persons a desire to keep up with or excel the Joneses is a strong motive for accepting new fashions. Advertisements, particularly those from mail-order houses, often admonish us to be the first on our block to own a particular product.

Environmental and cultural utility: The utility of a fashion, including its appropriateness to the social setting, is also important in its acceptance, growth, and decline (Miller 1985). Although not usually mentioned by psychologists, utility may be the major determiner of many fashions.

When the price of heating oil rose skyward in the 1970s, wood-burning stoves were rediscovered and came into vogue, and provisions for one were made in most new houses. The growth of wood-burning stoves' acceptance is typical of many fashions in which environmental needs play a role. There was a need for cheaper sources of heat. Wood stoves had been widely used years ago, so they carried with them a bit of nostalgia. They were being used unpretentiously by a small group of individuals, and that use was discovered. The stoves were redesigned to be more efficient and to be as attractive as a piece of prized furniture. They were widely advertised. Their price rose and they became status symbols, their users labeled as people familiar with the politics of world economics and concerned with the depletion of nonrenewable natural resources. Soon, however, users found that the stoves were not as neat, clean, and easy to use as had been expected. The price of wood went up, and wood smoke polluted the atmosphere. Besides, with so many families using wood stoves, they were no longer status symbols. The price of oil came down, at least temporarily. Many who had used oil heat had switched to cheaper natural gas. Wood stoves lost some of their social, psychological, and economic utility, and they have lost some of their fashion value as well.

The rise in the popularity of salad bars, especially in fast-food restaurants, follows a similar scenario, except that interest in salad bars is still high. People were already eating out, partly because many couples and parents were working outside the home and had less time to prepare meals and to clean up afterwards. The popularity of fast-food establishments had weakened the custom of eating full-course meals, so customers were willing to substitute one course—salads—for a full meal. At the same time, there was renewed interest in dieting and fitness, and dieters had eaten salads for years. The interest in fitness was coupled with nutritionists' criticism of fast foods for their high fat content and emphasis on eating lighter foods, especially vegetables and what was once called "rabbit food." There was also boredom with existing fast-food menus: hamburgers, fried chicken, pizza, and the like. Restaurants greatly expanded the variety of salads offered and included enough condiments to rival the seven sweets and seven sours of a Pennsylvania Dutch dinner. Customers' needs were met. Salads offer novelty (new combinations and exotic fruits and vegetables), health (brassicas and other green vegetables), and even nostalgia (cole slaw and carrot and raisin salads). Advertising has increased consumer awareness and added prestige. The place of salad bars in the future is unclear, but because they satisify nutritional, utilitarian, and social needs, they will probably continue in some form. Fads and fashions can become custom by adapting to prevailing conditions. Pancake houses are less popular now than they were thirty years ago, but many have survived by expanding their menus.

Different motivations can be identified for the rise of specific fads or fashions, especially when the fashions are not complex. For example, novelty is a motivation for eating sushi, nostalgia one for eating muffins, health one for eating broccoli, and prestige one for eating croissants. Usually, however, several motives work together. Both nostalgia and health are reasons for eating oatmeal, and although originally health may have been the motive for eating muffins, they have become so elaborate and filled with sugar that most likely the reasons are now novelty, nostalgia, and prestige. Finally, despite the presence of psychological needs and motives, it should be remembered that most of the foods simply taste good, and that may be the major reason why many food fads and fashions get started.

Fashions and Custom

Prevailing economic, environmental, and cultural conditions affect fashion, and insofar as custom is established fashion, they play a role in turning fashion into custom. The changes in the customary size of breakfasts and dinners demonstrate this. The large dinners of a century ago have given way to simpler ones. Our society was mostly rural at the time. Farms were not as specialized as they are now, so a greater variety of foods was available to those living on farms. Middle-class urban dwellers often had a cow, chickens, and a kitchen garden for milk, eggs, meat, and vegetables. The lack of refrigerators and freezers made it difficult to preserve portions of foods. One had to cook the whole chicken and could not store leftovers. People lived by the admonition "Waste not, want not" and so threw nothing out. In addition, individuals may have needed the energy supplied by larger meals. Many people were engaged in manual labor, and the working day was ten to twelve hours long, six days a week for both white- and blue-collar workers. Women seldom worked outside the home and were expected to prepare or oversee the preparation of large meals. Often there was a grandmother or maiden aunt to lend help, and children were required to assist in household chores, including meal preparation. Old cookbooks and articles on household management suggest that there was a move to make smaller dinners fashionable; but the switch to an urban economy, changes in family size, nutrition concepts, and food marketing and storage practices were probably more important in cultivating the fashion and establishing it as custom than was a desire for prestige.

Collective versus Individual Behavior

In collective behavior, the group, no matter how diffuse, consists of individuals doing the same thing at the same time. The individuals interact and their behaviors influence one another. The interaction, however, is limited. There is little or no mutual modification of behaviors in response to the needs and actions of others or to the needs and actions of the group. Rather, behavior is copied or imitated, and as suggested above, the copying usually follows a pattern: outsiders copy insiders and those lower in status copy those higher in status. In this process, personal face-to-face contact is not necessary. Although exposure to fashionable behaviors can be direct, they can also be learned through the media—television, magazines, newspapers, books, films—or by word of mouth.

Whenever individuals are influenced by others or by a group, either directly or by media intervention, there is a tendency to think that the group or others play a causal role. But thoughts and actions are always the thoughts and actions of individuals. The group itself has no mind and no nervous system. It can neither behave nor express ideas—only individuals can. Our susceptibility to suggestion and the complexity of our needs make us vulnerable to external influences, but those influences work as often, if not more often, for good as for ill. A great part of our socialization comes from copying and imitation (Bandura 1977), and most of us are certainly more good than bad.

PART 3

Food as a Complex Psychological Stimulus

CHAPTER 6

Taste

Food is a complex stimulus consisting of a number of physical characteristics such as shape, size, color, odor, taste, and temperature. Whenever food is physically present, each of these characteristics, singly or in combination, is represented in our experience as a sensory quality or sensation—the direct result of activity in the sensory areas of the brain via specialized receptor cells located in the retina of the eye, the taste buds of the tongue, and other locations. These sensations themselves are rather simple. In combination, they form the complex characteristics that professional chefs lump together under *appearance*, which is visual; *texture*, which refers to the way food feels in the mouth; and *flavor*, which includes both taste and smell.

Basic Tastes

Most of what is called taste is actually smell. The generally accepted tastes are salt, sweet, sour, and bitter. Other tastes such as alkaline, metallic, and "deliciousness" have been suggested (Boudreau 1979), but, with the possible exception of alkaline (Schiffman and Erickson 1971), there is little agreement that they really are tastes (Shiffman 1976). Their chemical bases are unclear, and specific receptors for them cannot be identified (McBurney and Gent 1979).

Tasting and Smelling as a Perceptual System

Most senses interact with one another, thus what is experienced through one sense is modified by activity in another. Nowhere is this interaction clearer than in the relation between taste and smell. The two together constitute a single perceptual system controlling the recognition, acceptance, enjoyment, and ingestion of food (Gibson 1966).

Only about 10 percent of what we think of as taste is actually taste. A piece of onion and a piece of apple of equal crispness will taste the same if the nose is held while eating them. On the basis of taste alone, clam and tomato juice are both salty and cannot be told apart. Canned orange juice is bitter and unrecognizable. When we have a cold and say that food has lost its taste, what we really mean is that it has lost its smell; taste is all that is left. Taste and smell working together produce what we call flavor. Their combination with texture allows us to know the qualities of food. But from a chemical and neurological point of view, taste and smell are very different senses. Psychologically, much more can be said about smell than about taste.

Physiology and Physics of Taste

Receptors: Most of the receptor cells for taste are in the taste buds (circumvalate papillae) of the tongue, but a few are in the throat and other parts of the mouth (Matlin 1983). Sweet substances are tasted on the tip and front edges of the tongue; salt, on the front; sour, along the middle edges; and bitter, toward the back and back edges. The center part of the tongue is relatively insensitive to tastes (Beidler 1978). Because of these differences in locations, on the first bite or sip of food, its sweet and salty qualities will be tasted before its sour and bitter ones. Saccharin, for example, tastes sweet at first, with the bitter taste occurring as the substance moves to the back of the tongue. A bitter aftertaste may linger if no other food is taken to stimulate other tastes or to wash away the saccharin. Chewing releases a continual flow of new particles to taste. Food eaten by individuals who chew with their front teeth tastes somewhat different than it does to those who chew with their molars.

In order for a substance to be tasted it must be dissolved at least partially. This is one of the functions of saliva. The combined tastes of a given food can be recognized only if the food touches all parts of the tongue. Obviously, this is ensured by chewing and by movement of the tongue or food while eating. If food is gulped, only a small amount of taste will be experienced.

Tasting may be necessary to stimulate the flow of gastric juices. In a classic case, an individual who was fed directly into the stomach did not get proper nourishment because the juices were not secreted unless he tasted the food first (Wilentz 1968). Of course, the sight, sound, or smell of food—a sizzling steak, for example—can activate the nervous system to secrete salivary enzymes which are needed to break down starches and other foods. Reactions to the temperature, smell, or taste of the first bite of food can enhance or inhibit such action.

Taste sensitivity: The concentration of a substance necessary for its presence to be detected (absolute threshold) differs with the taste and the substance (Woodworth and Schlosberg 1954). Of the different tastes, bitterness, to be detected, requires the weakest concentrations of substances. This may have adaptive value because many poisonous substances taste bitter. For quinine sulphate, we can detect 0.00003 grams dissolved in 100 cc of water. For sugar, 0.7 grams are required, but for saccharin it is only 0.0005 grams. The sour taste of hydrochloric acid is detected at 0.007 grams, and the saltiness of sodium chloride at 0.2 grams.

The difference threshold also varies with the taste and substance, but on average it is 20 percent. That means the concentration of a substance must be increased or decreased by approximately one-fifth in order for us to notice the change.

Sensitivity to tastes is highest in children and decreases slightly with age (Cowart 1981). There are also innate differences in sensitivity. Phenylthiocarbamide, known as PTC, tastes bitter to many individuals but is tasteless to about 30 percent of the U.S. and European populations and to 6 percent of American Indians (Kalmus 1952). Individual differences in taste sensitivity no doubt play a role in food preferences. The bitterness in spinach, turnips, and liver may go undetected by some but be enough to repel others.

The full intensity of a given taste is not experienced immediately but builds up to reach a peak in one-half to two seconds after the substance contacts the tongue. The time varies with the taste as well as with the substance. Citric acid, often added to soft drinks, gives a quick and sprightly sourness (Moskowitz 1978a). The sourness of malic (apple) acid, on the other hand, develops more slowly. It does not have a sprightly quality and would not be used to give soft drinks an initial punch. Bitterness takes the longest time to detect, quite aside from the fact of its receptors' location at the back of the tongue. Once a taste has reached its peak, the intensity seems to diminish slowly with continued stimulation. This adaptation occurs in controlled laboratory studies, but no change may occur in normal eating, because the food is moved around constantly so that no specific receptor has prolonged contact with it.

Taste stimuli: What chemical substances give rise to different tastes? The stimulus for the experience of sourness is an acid of some kind, or, more specifically, the hydrogen ion of dilute acid solutions. For salt, it is the sodium ion found in sodium chloride, or common table salt. Other sodium compounds also give a salty taste. However, in some compounds, the action of the sodium ion is inhibited, as in MSG (monosodium glutamate), so that they do not taste salty even though they contain a large amount of sodium. Neither sweet nor bitter is associated with a single chemical structure. Chemically dissimilar substances such as sugar, saccharin, alcohol, and the poison salt "sugar of lead" all taste sweet (Woodworth and Schlosberg 1954). Some bitter tastes are associated with alkaloids such as quinine, but not all bitter substances are alkaloids. In addition to their lack of characteristic stimuli, sweet and bitter have other similarities. Unlike salt and sour, there appear to be several different kinds of bitter and sweet tastes, involving different nerve fibers. Also, there are some chemical similarities in substances that taste sweet and bitter. These findings suggest that there may be some as yet unknown relation between sweet and bitter and that the description of something as bittersweet may have a basis in underlying physiology (Christman 1971). Certainly, the bitter and sweet tastes of chocolate seem to go together and are enjoyed by many.

Taste Modification
Mixing Tastes

Unlike odors or primary colors, tastes do not fuse or blend to form new taste compounds. Rather, they combine as mixtures much like a fruit salad in which the separate tastes keep their identities. This gives interest and variety and the impression of complexity to even simple foods. A ripe pear when savored yields all four tastes. Sweet-sour sauce is a sugar and an acid with odors and some texture added, but if the sweet and sour were not separately identifiable, the appeal would be lost. In taste combinations, the intensity of each is somewhat diminished, but no new compound emerges (McBurney 1978).

Taste Interactions

Although tastes do not fuse to form new tastes, they are modified in a variety of other ways. Cake and cookie batters taste sweet when the sugar granules are whole, but not when they are dissolved throughout the batter after cooking. Sweetness is more pronounced when foods are hot than when cold. A food that tastes just right while cooking may need more sugar after it has cooled. Sourness is also greater when food is warm. On the other hand, saltiness and particularly bitterness are less intense in heated foods. The cold paté which is now slightly bitter may have tasted fine when it was still hot chicken livers. For all tastes, the maximum sensitivity is usually when the substance is at body temperature (McBurney et al. 1973).

Color can affect perceived tastes, especially sweetness. Pale juices seem less sweet than more highly colored ones (Schutz 1954), although too intense a color can have a negative effect. Fruit that looks unripe and sweet corn with large kernels also seem less sweet, even when they aren't. This is probably due to an expectation based on past experience: pale fruit and large-kerneled corn usually are less sweet so we expect them to be, and this expectation affects their apparent taste.

Adaptation and Taste Modifiers

Because of adaptation, a drink that tastes sour or sweet at first may seem less so as we continue drinking it. Sour foods taste more sour after sweet ones. To some persons, milk tastes odd after they have eaten asparagus or liver. Some toothpastes contain a detergent (sodium laurel sulfate) that makes orange juice taste less sweet and more sour and bitter (Bartoshuk 1980). On the other hand, berries of the African plant *Synsepalum dulcificum* make sour substances taste sweet. Some individuals report that water seems sweet after they have eaten artichokes. MSG supposedly enhances taste or perhaps aroma (but a dash of nutmeg will do the same without the added sodium). For some individuals, salt increases apparent sweetness (Charley 1982). Sugar reduces the bitterness of caffeine and can reduce, but not eliminate, the sourness of fruit pies. Chewing the leaves of the plant *Gymnema sylvestre* makes sugar "taste" like sand (Beidler 1966).

Taste adaptation is fairly complex (Christman 1971). For example, adaptation to the bitterness of quinine makes one more sensitive to saltiness and sourness, but not to sweetness. Adaptation to sour substances reduces the sourness of all sour substances, but adaptation to a salty substance reduces only the saltiness of that substance.

Taste Preferences

Humans, like many lower animals, have an inborn preference for sweet and slightly salty substances and an aversion to sour and bitter ones. This may have some life-preserving value since many poisonous substances taste bitter and most naturally sweet ones are not harmful. However, actual preferences depend on the concentrations of the substances being tasted. Adults find very weak bitter solutions pleasant, otherwise tonic water and bitter lemon would have no market as mixers. Generally, sweetness and saltiness increase in pleasantness up to a point and then level off and decline. Sourness and bitterness are more likely to be neutral or mildly pleasant at low concentrations before becoming unpleasant as the concentrations increase (Moskowitz 1978a).

Intense concentrations of any taste can cause pain or nausea. Nux vomica and quassia, both of which have a bitter taste, have been prescribed to induce hunger in underweight individuals by increasing the flow of saliva and gastric juices. In strong concentrations, bitter and salty liquids are emetics. The body seems to react to intense tastes of any kind. Years ago at syrup-making time, rural children used to make snow candy by throwing boiling maple syrup over the snow outside the sugar house. Often they would gorge themselves on this until their stomachs rebelled by throwing it all up. The children experienced no nausea and would want more of the candy immediately afterward.

Tastes and Food Preferences

Because of the limited number of tastes, they contribute much less than odor and texture to variations in food preferences and acceptance, so long as the taste concentrations are within a suitable range. Odor, texture, mouthfeel, and perhaps even appearance are more important. Therefore, not much can be said relating tastes to classes of foods. Generally, sweet substances are preferred in desserts. Saltiness goes with soups and entrees, and bitterness with vegetables. Sourness can be liked in any category including salads and desserts. Taste combinations are especially enjoyed. Of course, the liking for any taste depends on the particular food in question as well as on its associations and the context in which it is served or eaten.

CHAPTER 7
Odor

Odor is by far the most important contributor to the flavor of food. The contributions of taste, texture, and appearance are insignificant by comparison. Without aroma, food would still feel hot or cold, soft or crunchy, but its taste would be limited almost entirely to salt, sweet, sour, or bitter.

Odor has far-reaching effects on our lives not only for eating and self-preservation, but also for a variety of social activities, perhaps including our attraction or aversion to other people (Cain 1978b). Yet, it remains somewhat a mystery psychologically and physiologically.

Physiology and Physics of Smell

For a substance to be smelled, it must be in a gaseous form, that is, partially dissolved in air. Air containing odor molecules from outside the body enters the nasal cavity from the nose or mouth. If a substance is already in the mouth, air containing odor molecules from the substance reaches the nasal cavity from the mouth and throat. Through diffusion, air bathes the lining of the upper nasal cavity where the olfactory skin, or epithelium, is located. Only about 2 percent of the odorous molecules taken in actually reach the epithelium (Mozell 1971). Within this epithelium are the smell receptors—approximately 5 million in all. The receptor cells are covered with a thin layer of mucus; they are activated when particles of the odorant in the air are either dissolved in or pass through this liquid medium, or, perhaps, absorb heat from the epithelium. The inability to smell when we have a cold is due to blockage of the nasal cavity or to excessive thickness of the mucus coating, which inhibits receptor activity. From the receptors, neural impulses pass along the olfactory nerve to the olfactory bulb of the brain and then to other parts of the brain.

Sensitivity

Humans can distinguish an estimated 20,000 different odor qualities and 10 intensities of each (Mueller 1965). This makes 200,000 odor impressions. Some estimates are even higher, going up to 16 million or even more (Charley 1982), which is, perhaps, too high. In this respect, the sense of smell is superior to taste and may be as good as or better than hearing or color vision. We can distinguish approximately 340,000 tones and perhaps 10,000,000 color qualities (Stevens and Davis 1938). In taste, the number of discriminable qualities is difficult to determine, but one estimate suggests it is about the same as for odor (Beidler 1966). Humans are very sensitive to minute concentrations of odorous substances. In some cases we can detect concentrations that are 20,000 times weaker than what is needed for taste (Bartley 1958). Dogs are 100 times more sensitive to some odors than are humans; both dogs and pigs can locate truffles underground, using smells that humans cannot detect.

Thresholds: The amount of material needed in order to detect an odor (the detection, or absolute, threshold) varies with the substance. It takes less than 0.0000001 milligrams of artificial musk in a liter of air to be detected. That is an amount equal to less than one ten-billionth of a peanut (Matlin 1983). On the other hand, there must be 5.83 milligrams of ether in a liter of air before it can be detected. The amount of material needed also varies for the same substance produced by different manufacturers. One brand of vanilla may be more potent than another. Thresholds also depend on how the odorant is presented or sniffed. The size of the threshold can be as much as 10,000 times smaller or larger depending on the method used (Mozell 1971). Further, adaptation to odors is very rapid, and a second sniff will require a stronger concentration than the first, if it is to be detected. With butyl alcohol, for example, the concentration must be 200 times stronger on the second presentation (Moncrieff 1966b).

Substances used in flavorings and perfumes usually require low concentrations; for vanillin, it may be as small as 0.0000000002 milligrams per liter of air (Charley 1982). They should also be ones whose odors are not easily dissipated, although this is more important for perfumes than for foods. In fact, an after-odor in some foods is undesirable—garlic and onions, for example. The flavor of a piece of pie should stay with us while it is being eaten, but foods that are eaten in bits and pieces interrupted with bites of other foods should not have odors that linger to mask the flavors of the other foods. Of course, if properly done, a sequence of odors can produce a subtle mixture that adds interest and complexity to the meal. For some foods, perhaps the best flavorings are those that are apparent while the food is being chewed but dissipate quickly after chewing stops. Some compromise and common sense should be used, however. If all lingering odors were eliminated, we would lose the enticing odor of bakeries and the savory smell of pot roast cooking on the stove. Many of the pleasant kitchen smells are already disappearing because of microwaving, which cooks foods so fast that there is no time for their odors to fill the room.

In spite of our sensitivity to odors, humans are not very good at detecting changes in odor intensity. In the artificial conditions of the laboratory, the amount by which an odor has to be increased or decreased in order for the change to be detected (the difference threshold) may be close to 4 percent (Engen 1982), but in the real world of everyday living, it is more like 20 to 30 percent of original amount (Matlin 1983). This is about 5 percent higher than for taste. If one teaspoon of vanilla extract has been used, another quarter of a teaspoon should make the flavor stronger.

Individual differences in odor sensitivity: Odor sensitivity may be affected by age (Engen 1982). Newborn infants seem to be able to detect odors, and infants as young as two days old may be able to tell some of them apart. It has long been believed that there is a loss of sensitivity in the elderly, and this has been found, but not by all researchers. It is clear, however, that the elderly find it harder to identify foods by their odors, but naming odors is a problem at all ages ("I know the smell, but just can't place it"). It has been estimated that the number of substances one can identify with a single sniff varies from only six to twenty-two, but if the odors used are ones commonly found in everyday objects, the average rises to thirty-six (Cain 1979). The poorer performance of older persons may have as much to do with changes in cognition or general health as with changes in odor sensitivity. For all practical purposes, whether or not there is an actual loss in *sensitivity* does not matter. Many elderly persons are less able to detect and recognize odors.

Individual differences also play a role in odor detection and difference thresholds. Among normal healthy adults, one person may be a hundred times more sensitive than another to a particular odor (Cain 1978b). This creates problems for flavoring foods. What may be a hint of anise to one person may be entirely lacking to another and too powerful to still another. Further, some odors that are pleasant at low concentrations become unpleasant at higher ones, and a pleasant fragrance may be unpleasant to a more sensitive nose.

The reasons for individual differences are complex. Some may be due to differences in neural sensitivity, shallowness or depth of breathing, structure of the nasal cavity, or mucus secretions that block or impede the activity of the odor receptors. Others may be due to the degree to which individuals pay attention to odors. Just as some people are more responsive to colors than to sounds or to painting than to music, so may others be more responsive to odors. Some individuals eat without thinking while others take the time to notice and savor their food.

Odor Stimuli

There is little definite knowledge about the chemical nature of substances that arouse the sense of smell in particular ways, except that they are usually organic compounds and have molecular weights between 15 and 300 (Cain 1978a). This tells us little other than the range within which molecules will give smell sensations. In vision, we know that light with wavelengths between 400 and 700 millimicrons will be visible, but we also know what colors go with specific wavelengths. Some research shows that amines of low molecular weights smell fishy or urinous and those of high weights smell garlicky or sulfurous. Most compounds that contain sulfur and some that contain nitrogen have a vile smell (Cain 1978b).

One of the more recent views suggests that the chemical composition of a substance is largely irrelevant for its odor. Instead, the shape and size of the molecules are important, with molecules of similar shapes giving rise to the same odor experience (Amoore 1970). This is the stereochemical theory of olfaction, in which it is proposed that there are seven basic odors, five of which depend on molecular shape and two of which—pungent and putrid—depend on chemical charges within the molecules. The five shape-based primaries and their standards and shapes are: camphora-ceous (camphor or mothballs—spherical), ethereal (ether or cleaning fluid—rod-shaped), musky (musk—disk-shaped), floral (roses—kite- or disk-shaped with a flexible tail), and minty (peppermint—wedge-shaped).

One of the major criticisms of the theory is that some substances with molecules of similar shapes do not smell the same (Beets 1978). The theory has been expanded to include molecular profiles or orientations and to incorporate an early but still current view that specific odors depend on the rate of intramolecular vibration, which is shown partly by the rate at which the odorous gases absorb heat from the olfactory epithelium (Cain 1978a; Wright 1966).

Classification of Odors

Basic colors, shapes, and tastes are known, and most colors and forms can be produced by various combinations of a few primary ones. For odors, there is no agreement as to what is basic or even if basic odors exist (Hainer et al. 1954), although several dozen different lists have been pro-posed (Harper et al., *Odour description,* 1968). One of the earliest classifica-tions was made by Aristotle, who proposed sweet, pungent, harsh, sour, succulent, and fetid (Cain 1978a). A more commonly used classification, based on medicinal substances then in use, was made by Linnaeus, the Swedish botanist, in 1752 (Cain 1978a; Moncrieff 1966b; Woodworth and Schlosberg 1954). His basic classes of odors and their standards were: aromatic (carnation), fragrant (lily), ambrosial (musk), alliaceous or oniony (garlic), hircine or goaty (valerian), repulsive (stinkbugs), and nauseating (carrion). This was expanded in 1895 by the Dutch physiologist Hendrik Zwaardemaker by the addition of two classes—ethereal (fruity) and burned—and several subclasses to the aromatic, fragrant, and alliaceous categories.

In 1916, Hans Henning proposed a system with six classes of odors—fragrant (rose), ethereal or fruity (lemon), resinous (pine), spicy (cloves), putrid (feces), and burned (tar)—which he arranged in a three-dimensional smell prism. Supposedly, any odor could be identified by its resemblance to one or more of the six salient odors, but the system has been criticized, partly for questions of its validity and partly for its difficulty.

A more workable system, based on four odor components—fragrant, acid, burned, and caprylic or goaty—was developed by E. C. Crocker and L. F. Henderson in 1927 (Crocker 1945; Woodworth and Schlosberg 1954). Most psychologists believe there are more than four basic odors, and there has been some criticism of Crocker and Henderson's system on the grounds that untrained judges do not give consistent results (Ross and Harriman 1949), but it has had great practical value for describing or rating the odor characteristics of a wide variety of substances, particularly in the perfume industry. In order to evaluate an odor, eight standard intensities of the four basic odors are used. By systematically comparing an odor with each of the standards, numerical values can be given to the odor. Thus, a rose might be 7 fragrant, 3 acid, 2 burned, and 3 caprylic. Standard vanillin is 7122, and coffee is 7683 (Charley 1982).

A system that is even more useful for identifying the odor characteristics of foods was developed by Harper, Land, Griffiths, and Bate-Smith in 1968 (Harper et al., *Odour description*, 1968; Harper et al., *Odour qualities*, 1968). From over 300 terms used to describe smells, they systematically selected 44 that were particularly meaningful and well understood. That list is shown in table 7-1 (Harper et al., *Odour qualities*, 1968). In using the procedure to evaluate the odors of foods, standard or comparison samples are not used. Rather, the food item is sipped or sniffed and then rated on a six-point scale for each of the qualities represented by the 44 terms. The procedure has been criticized for not using standard comparison stimuli, but the fact is that there are very few odorous substances that represent only a single quality. Most foods and natural substances have several complex odors. One has little difficulty knowing what fishy or yeasty means, but any food that smells fishy, yeasty, or musty will also give a number of other olfactory impressions. The system has the advantage of using enough terms with clear meanings to convey in detail the olfactory characteristics of a wide variety of foods.

The Modification of Odors
Interaction of the Senses

Food is never a gas. Whether solid or liquid, it has substance that activates various receptors and gives impressions of taste, texture, and smell. However, a variety of sensations ordinarily accompany the odor component itself because there are receptors in the nose for touch, pain, warmth, and cold and receptors in the throat for taste, all of which may be activated

TABLE 7-1. Score sheet for odor qualities

Please score numbers on the scale:	Absent 0	Slightly 1	2	Moderately 3	4	Extremely 5
P						
Aromatic	0	1	2	3	4	5
Meaty (cooked)	0	1	2	3	4	5
Sickly	0	1	2	3	4	5
Musty, earthy, mouldy	0	1	2	3	4	5
Sharp, pungent, acid	0	1	2	3	4	5
Camphor-like	0	1	2	3	4	5
Light	0	1	2	3	4	5
Heavy	0	1	2	3	4	5
Cool, cooling	0	1	2	3	4	5
Warm	0	1	2	3	4	5
Metallic	0	1	2	3	4	5
Q						
Fragrant	0	1	2	3	4	5
Sweaty	0	1	2	3	4	5
Almond-like	0	1	2	3	4	5
Burnt, smoky	0	1	2	3	4	5
Herbal, green, cut grass, etc.	0	1	2	3	4	5
Etherish, anaesthetic	0	1	2	3	4	5
Sour, acid, vinegar, etc.	0	1	2	3	4	5
Like blood, raw meat	0	1	2	3	4	5
Dry, powdery	0	1	2	3	4	5
Like ammonia	0	1	2	3	4	5
Disinfectant, carbolic	0	1	2	3	4	5
R						
Fruity (citrus)	0	1	2	3	4	5
Fruity (other)	0	1	2	3	4	5
Putrid, foul, decayed	0	1	2	3	4	5
Woody, resinous	0	1	2	3	4	5
Musk-like	0	1	2	3	4	5
Soapy	0	1	2	3	4	5
Garlic, onion	0	1	2	3	4	5
Animal	0	1	2	3	4	5
Vanilla-like	0	1	2	3	4	5
Faecal (dung-like)	0	1	2	3	4	5
Floral	0	1	2	3	4	5
S						
Oily, fatty	0	1	2	3	4	5
Like mothballs	0	1	2	3	4	5
Like petrol, solvent	0	1	2	3	4	5
Cooked vegetables	0	1	2	3	4	5
Sweet	0	1	2	3	4	5
Fishy	0	1	2	3	4	5
Spicy	0	1	2	3	4	5
Paint-like	0	1	2	3	4	5
Rancid	0	1	2	3	4	5
Minty, peppermint	0	1	2	3	4	5
Sulphurous	0	1	2	3	4	5

Reprinted by permission from: Harper, R., Land, D. G., Griffiths, N. M., and Bate-Smith, E. C. (1968). Odour qualities: A glossary of usage. *British Journal of Psychology*, 59: 231–52.

when air is inhaled through the nose or mouth. Probably as many as 75 percent of all odors give sensations besides odor (Woodworth 1938). Among these are sharp or prickly (ammonia and vinegar), cold (menthol and garlic), sweet (chloroform), warm (cloves), and sour (buttermilk). There are even responses of tickle and itch from the smell of pepper.

Interaction of the senses also takes place at higher brain centers. For this reason it has been suggested that we should speak of the senses as a perceptual system, rather than as a collection of individual senses, which as a whole gives us information about the world around us (Gibson 1966). This is particularly true of taste, smell, and texture, which work together to give us knowledge of food's palatability and pleasantness as well as its sensory qualities and perhaps nutritional values.

The way in which we use descriptive words supports the idea of a single system of interacting senses. The following qualities have been suggested for odors: loose-tight, light-heavy, smooth-rough, soft-hard, thin-thick, sharp-dull, bright-dull, lively-inert, surfacey-deep, and small-large (Hazzard 1930). Many of the terms apply equally well to tastes, sounds, colors, and textures, as well as to touch and pain.

The perceived intensities of odors can be enhanced or diminished by activity in other senses. The effect is pronounced with changes in color that affect both taste and smell. Odors can also be used to enhance an existing flavor, as by the addition of almond extract to cherry pie. Odors also compensate for the lack of other seasonings. Spicy foods need less or no salt to be equally flavorful, and appropriate seasonings allow a reduction of sugar without any loss in flavor.

Although flavor is modified by the presence of other sensations, changes in smell occur as a direct result of adaptation and odor-mixing, without changes in other sensations.

Adaptation

Adaptation, discussed earlier, refers to the fact that a stimulus seems to get weaker as we continue to be exposed to it. It happens in all senses but is most noticeable with odors. For odor, the decline occurs at the rate of about 2.5 percent per second until the odor has only about 30 percent of its original intensity (Cain 1978b). These are average figures; the decline is faster and to a lower level for weak odors than for strong ones. Since adaptation occurs at different rates for different odors, the smell of substances with complex odors, including most foods, may undergo several changes as first one and then another of the component odors adapts out. Although adaptation is never complete, an odor can become so weak that we no longer notice it. Exposure and adaptation to one odor decrease sensitivity to other odors with the result that other odors, particularly weak ones, may go undetected. Delicate aromas that normally would be smelled in foods may be missed, especially if they follow strongly flavored foods.

The pattern of service should be from weaker to stronger odors unless there is a break to allow for recovery from adaptation. Serving salad after the main course allows time for recovery from strong meat flavors so that delicate desserts can be appreciated. There have been a few reports of facilitation, in which smelling an odor makes a following odor smell stronger. This seems to be limited to a few alcohols in laboratory settings, but it is possible that very weak odors sensitize individuals to other odors (Engen 1982).

Odor-Mixing

The laws of color mixture are well established. With light, complementary colors (those opposite each other on the color circle) combine to produce a neutral gray. Any other two colors produce a color somewhere between them. For paints, only the second principle applies. When tastes are combined, the resulting taste usually retains the full characteristics of the separate tastes, such as bitter and sweet or sweet and sour. There are a few exceptions: for example, sugar reduces sourness and saltiness, and salt reduces acidity (Charley 1982).

When odors are mixed, almost anything can happen, depending on the odorants, their intensities, and the manner of mixing (Engen 1982; Woodworth and Schlosberg 1954). There are at least six different possible results. (1) Most commonly, the odors will fuse or blend to produce a single odor; this effect is greatest for odors that resemble each other. (2) Alternation or successive smelling may occur, in which one odor stands out and then another; this is more likely to occur with very different odors. (3) The component odors may be smelled simultaneously but each will be recognized. (4) One odor may mask or block out another, especially if one is much stronger. (5) Odors may neutralize each other so that no odor is smelled, although this result is questioned by some researchers (Woodworth 1938). (6) It has been reported that adding a below-threshold concentration to an above-threshold concentration of odors makes the above-threshold odor smell stronger, but this effect is extremely rare. One other point regarding mixtures is relevant: generally, a mixture of odors does not smell as strong as the sum of the intensities of the individual odors in the mixture (Cain 1978b; Engen 1982).

Odor Preferences

Preferences for many foods, especially those without distinguishing appearance, taste, or texture, are largely a function of their odors. Yet there are no systematic studies of food-odor preferences. What are the preference ratings for the odors of common foods? How would those ratings compare with ratings of the same foods based on appearance, taste, and texture? Perhaps raspberries are liked mainly for their smell, green beans for their texture, lemon tarts for their taste, and gelatin swirls for their appearance. In the absence of appropriate studies, we have to get what information we can from more general odor-preference studies in which researchers tend to use pure or artificial essences or odorants isolated from their natural sources and from other components.

Pleasantness and Preferences

In many studies, no distinction is made between odor preference and odor pleasantness. The two ratings usually coincide, but not always. For example, the *Mollis* azalea has a skunk-like odor that may be rated more unpleasant than the smell of tulips. Nevertheless, a person may prefer azaleas to tulips, especially if the flowers are smelled in their natural settings. To some people black walnuts smell unpleasant as an isolated odor, but are liked as a flavor for cakes, candies, and ice cream. The appearance, tastes, and textures of foods as well as the associations one has with them all affect preferences and can also affect perceived odors. Consequently, the pleasantness ratings of pure isolated odors may not be the same as ratings obtained from seeing, tasting, and sniffing actual foods.

Various studies of odor preferences show considerable overall agreement; this is true despite differences in detailed findings, which come about usually because of differences in the procedures of presenting the odorants, instructing the participants, or recording and analyzing the results.

Moncrieff's Preference Studies

Perhaps the most extensive preference studies were carried out in England by R. W. Moncrieff over a period of several years (Moncrieff 1966b). Like most researchers, he equated preference and pleasantness. In one study, 132 different odors were arranged in order of preference by 12 individuals. Each person ranked at least 118 of the 132 odorants. The method of paired comparisons was used, with each odor being compared with every other odor. Both natural and artificial odorants were used. The results for 50 of the odors most relevant for food flavor are shown in table 7-2.

In a second study, 10 odorants were ranked by 559 people. The individuals were simply asked to rank the sniffed odors in order of preference. In both studies, the data were analyzed to identify differences based on age, sex, and personality (introversion-extroversion). Moncrieff compared his results with those of other researchers and presented the findings in 124 conclusions, many of which are of interest to foodservice practices. The following is a summary of the results.

Odors that are strongly liked or disliked are liked or disliked by almost everyone. There is more variation in children's preferences and in the middle preference ranges that make up most odors. Agreement in the

TABLE 7-2. **Rankings of food-related odors from among 132 odorants studied**

Odorant	Type of odor	Rank
Fresh strawberries	Strawberries	2nd
Honeysuckle flowers	Floral, rich, honey	7th
Raspberry flavoring essence	Fruity, very true	9th
Sweet orange oil	Orange, light and very natural	10th
Lemon flavoring essence	Lemon, slightly bitter	11th
Meadowsweet, flower	Rich floral, honey note	12th
Peppermint flavoring essence	Peppermint	13th
Strawberry flavoring essence	Strawberry, very sweet	14th
Heliotrope, flower	Cherry pie	15th
Lemon flavoring essence	Lemon, slightly sweet	16th
Banana flavoring essence	Banana	17th
Spearmint oil	Spearmint	18th
Garden mint, fresh	Minty	21st
Vanilla flavoring essence	Vanilla	21st
Cinnamon leaf oil	Cinnamon, light, spicy	27th
Orange flavoring essence	Orange, a shade lemony	28th
Citral	Powerful lemony, a little sweet	30th
Cinnamon bark oil	Cinnamon, heavy, sweet, spicy	32nd
Bay leaf, dried	Reminiscent of curry, bitter, hint of roasting coffee	33rd
Ribes (flowering current), fresh leaf	Fresh, green, fruity, like mint and black-current	34th
Strawberry aldehyde	Strawberry with acid note	35th
Vanillin 100% ex eugenol	Vanilla	37th
Almond flavoring essence	Almonds	40th
Lemongrass oil	Lemony like citral, but a little smoky	42nd
Isoeugenol	Spicy, sour, hint of cloves	43rd
Eugenol	Cloves	45th
Parsley, fresh	Parsley.	46th
Amyl butyrate, ex technical amyl alcohol	Powerful, fruity	50th
Coconut flavoring essence	Coconut	51st
Chives, fresh	Onion, but milder and fresher	52nd
Onion, raw, cut	Onion	54th
Terpinolene	Bitter, lemony, hint of hyacinth	55th
Tonka beans, tincture in benzyl alcohol	Nutty, sweet, some coumarin	56th
Heliotropine crystals	Floral, cherry pie	58th
Oil of citronella, Ceylon	Sweet, spicy, floral	70th

(*continued*)

TABLE 7-2. **Rankings of food-related odors from among 132 odorants studied (continued)**

Odorant	Type of odor	Rank
Allyl caproate	Pineapple, coarse and strong	74th
Methyl salicylate	Wintergreen	82nd
Veratrol	Like thyme, but sweeter	83rd
Peach synthetic concentrate	Peach	87th
Ethyl acetate	Mild "rum and butter"	94th
Benzaldehyde, redistilled	Nutty, almonds	97th
Undecalactone	Ripe peaches, nutty	99th
Ethyl acetate	Fruity	104th
Sour milk	Sour	110th
Rape oil	Light oily, nutty	112th
Benzylamine	Bitter, fishy, sharp	114th
Acetic acid, glacial	Vinegarish, sour	115th
Herring oil	Oily, fishy	121st
Triethylamine	Ammoniacal, organic, fishy	129th
p-Chlorothiophenol	Pungent, burnt, sweetish	130th

Excerpted by permission from: Moncrieff, R. W. (1966). *Odour preferences*. New York: Wiley. © Blackie & Son, Ltd., Glasgow.

middle ranges improves as the odors become even slightly unpleasant. This means people are more in agreement about the odors they find unpleasant than those they find pleasant.

Natural flower and fruit odors are most liked, with children liking fruity odors more than adults do. Strong concentrations of odors usually are not liked. Natural odors are not very strong, and they are also complex, consisting of shades and nuances. This complexity may make them more appealing than synthetics or single, pure odors even at low concentrations.

Age is a more important determiner of odor preferences than is sex, but there are some sex differences. These are most pronounced between the ages of fifteen and forty, the most fertile years, but show up even in eight-year-olds. Sex differences in preferences continue into old age if the preference is shown by men, but they tend to disappear after age forty if shown by women.

Adult women seem to be more responsive to some male odors during their menstrual periods (Engen 1982), and although they usually find the smell of Exaltolide strong and unpleasant, during pregnancy they find that it smells fairly pleasant (Wright 1964). Musks are generally ranked higher by men than by women. If males and females show marked differences in their rating of an odor, it is probably the males who like it better. At the time of Moncrieff's studies (1965), culinary odors were more preferred by women, but this may have changed now that more men are preparing and cooking more meals.

Fruit, flower, and essential-oil smells such as sweet orange or lavender are liked equally by men and women, but men prefer complex to simple flower smells. There is no report with respect to sex differences in preferences for simple or complex food odors, but if the same complexity differences occur, that might partly account for the greater number of male than female chefs.

All individuals prefer natural materials to synthetic ones, but children are much more accepting of synthetic flavors than are adults. Fruity smells are preferred maximally at ten to eleven years. Both these points are confirmed by the liking of many children for candies and ices. Children dislike oily smells and are less fond of sweet flower smells than are adults. They also seem to like some nutty smells (almond and coconut) better, but they dislike alcohol more. Children up to four or five years old may be more tolerant of unpleasant odors such as sweat and feces than are older children and adults (Engen 1982). Young adults, fifteen to twenty-five years old, rate onion and chive smells higher than do children or older adults. They also rate alcohol higher, but still relatively low. Musky and fruity smells are rated higher by those over twenty-five.

Moncrieff found that personality or temperament had little effect on most odor preferences, but a few trends were discernible. When introvert and extrovert preferences differed, the introvert preferences for unpleasant odors and the extrovert preferences for pleasant odors were more like those of children. Also, when the two groups differed, the introverts were more likely to like the odor. A different study showed that individuals who preferred bright, highly colored modern art also preferred stronger, more pungent odors (Eysenck 1944). Additional studies examining a wider range of personality characteristics are needed.

Food Odors and Food Preferences

Standard odor-preference studies suggest only a few very general principles relevant to food preferences. For example, we prefer fruity and floral odors of moderate intensity. However, there are so many inconsistencies and exceptions to the general rule that it is not very useful in predicting what foods will be liked or disliked. Attar of roses is quite pleasant, but we certainly would not want fried eggs flavored with it. We do not like sour milk to drink, but we may enjoy yogurt. Burned vegetables are unpleasant; so is the smell of vinegar, but both odors are often desired in barbecued foods.

Not only is there a lack of studies showing what odors we like in what foods, but also there are no studies comparing the odors of specific foods. Is the smell of corn more pleasant than that of peas? What about the smell of tomatoes compared with that of veal cutlets or chocolate cake? Is the odor of apples preferred to that of peaches, or the odor of Granny Smith apples to that of Red Delicious apples?

No doubt some food-odor preferences are matters of individual taste, but general patterns begin to emerge when they are examined with reference to classes or categories of foods rather than single food items. There are clear differences among most menu-item categories. The relations are far from absolute, but they are much clearer here than in taste, texture, or appearance.

Main Dishes

As pure odors, many of the smells occurring with meat and other main-dish foods are unpleasant. Odors such as fatty, smoky, burned, fleshy, meaty, and fishy are consistently ranked low in pleasantness. They would be repulsive in vegetables and desserts, but are often highly prized in main dishes. Many of the odors used in ethnic cooking, such as dried fish or fermented beans in Chinese foods, are extremely unpleasant, at least to Westerners, but in combinations or mixtures they make appealing main courses. (It would be interesting to know if the individual odors are considered unpleasant in China also.)

Odors that are highly unpleasant in themselves are not often found outside main-course foods. Two of the most unpleasant cooking odors are boiled cabbage and sauerkraut, which resemble the smell of rotten eggs, an odor always rated among the most unpleasant. Both are vegetables but are rarely served as vegetable side dishes, although sauerkraut accompanies Christmas roast goose on Maryland's Eastern Shore. Rather, they are served usually as integral parts of a main course such as corned beef or with various sausages or casseroles. Garlic, which is considered an unpleasant odor, is commonly used with meats, less often with vegetables, soups, or salads, and never with desserts.

Vinegar and lemon juice (acetic acid and citric acid) have peculiar positions. They are commonly used in main dishes such as sauerbraten and barbecued foods, but they are used also in salads, to flavor vegetables, to accompany other foods in a relish, and in desserts such as lemon mousse and vinegar or lemon pie. Lemons smell pleasant; vinegar does not (cider vinegar smells like rotting apples). But both also have a sour taste, and that is probably the reason for their widespread use. Sweet-sour is a favored taste in all menu categories.

Vegetables and Soups

Unpleasant odors are less often preferred in vegetables, and vegetables with unpleasant odors—broccoli, cabbage, leeks, onions, and parsnips—are among the least liked. In soups, an unpleasant meat, fish, or vegetable odor is less acceptable. A good fish chowder or onion soup has a smell less strong than that of either fish or onion. For soups, the odors of meats and vegetables, whether pleasant or unpleasant, are weakened by dilution with liquids or by mixture with other components. When soup is served as a main course, however, it is made more hearty, with characteristics resembling main dishes. Few of the odors ranked as really pleasant are ever found in soups, vegetables, or main dishes except as the gentlest hints of seasoning.

Salads

With salads, odor preferences begin to change. For meat, seafood, or vegetable salads, the principle that applies to soups also holds. Perhaps that is why consumers accept the economy of getting either soup or salad with their meals. Lighter and more pleasant odors are preferred, something that often is accomplished by using lettuce or mixing the main item with others that have pleasant or very weak unpleasant odors. For other salads there is a marked transition from the use of main foods with unpleasant odors to ones that are clearly pleasant. Fruit and gelatin salads are examples, but even those are modified by the use of dressings or other items with touches of unpleasant odors.

Desserts

Truly pleasant odors are reserved almost exclusively for desserts. These are the fragrant odors of flowers and fruits and some of the more delicate spices. Of course, these fragrances are used in soups, salads, and main dishes, but, with the exception of some salads, they are used only as complements, and not as the dominant odor. In addition to having more pleasant odors, desserts as a group usually have weaker and lighter odors.

Considering the discussions above, if we think of food odors on scales of pleasant-unpleasant, weak-intense (delicate-strong), and light-heavy, a general principle emerges: the farther removed an item is from the main dish, or the more unlike the main dish it is, the more pleasant, weaker, and lighter the preferred odors will be. On all three scales, with "5" as most pleasant, weakest, and lightest, the order of rank is: 1—main dishes, 2—vegetables, 3—soups, 4—salads, and 5—desserts. Any variations occurring because of specific foods will usually involve shifts between soups and vegetables, and between salads and desserts. If the older order of service is used, only soups are out of sequence: soup (3), main dish (1), vegetable (2), salad (4), and dessert (5).

Meals are arranged to achieve an overall balance, and with lighter or heavier main dishes items in other categories ordinarily would be adjusted up or down so that the preference ranks would still apply. Perhaps the greatest possibility for exception is in desserts, where a dessert with a heavy, strong, and unpleasant odor or one with a light and pleasant odor might be used even if the rest of the meal were in the opposite direction.

Reasons for Food-Odor Preferences

It seems reasonable to believe that some odors are strongly liked or disliked because they or the objects from which they come are helpful or harmful to us, but whether preferences have innate survival value is difficult to ascertain, particularly since it is not even known whether there are unlearned preferences present at birth. Newborn babies are able to detect odors, but do not seem to discriminate between odors that adults find pleasant or unpleasant (Engen 1982). Preferences are present by the time the child is a few weeks old, and maximum liking and disliking occur when children are about ten years of age (Moncrieff 1966a), but it is unclear whether this is due to maturation or experience—if only the experience of being exposed to various odors.

Body and physiological needs can produce fluctuations or short-term changes in the pleasantness and unpleasantness of odors. If we have a hangover, the smell of beer can be nauseating. Most foods smell more attractive if we are hungry and lose their pleasantness if we have overeaten. In fact, researchers have shown that the rated pleasantness of a food decreases after eating (Barker 1982), but how much of this is due to changes in odor preferences is unknown.

It would be easy to cite previous learning or experience as the reason for odor preferences, but the fact that there is high agreement among individuals as to what odors are liked and disliked suggests these preferences are not learned, at least not idiosyncratically. Learning and social custom or suggestion are more likely to be effective in the middle ranges where preferences are neither very strong nor very weak. It is a basic learning principle that neutral or ambiguous stimuli come to take on values or meaning through association with stronger, more meaningful ones. Thus, relatively neutral odors might be made more pleasant or unpleasant through association with pleasant or unpleasant situations, while strongly liked or disliked odors would be unaffected by such experiences.

This conclusion is supported by what we know about odors and food preferences. Liked food may contain unpleasant odors, and the pure odor, if isolated, remains unpleasant in spite of that liking. Pleasant odors may be more affected by associations, because people are less certain of their likes than of their dislikes (Moncrieff 1966b). This means that even strongly positive preferences may be somewhat ambiguous, and it will be easier for previously pleasant odors to be made unpleasant than for unpleasant odors to be made pleasant. This is confirmed by everyday experience. We may be repelled by the smell of a once-favored food by a single experience of illness after eating it. None of this means, however, that the pleasantness or unpleasantness of even moderately liked or disliked odors is necessarily or usually learned. More research is needed before that question can be answered.

Although a direct relation between associations and the pleasantness of odors has not been established, odors are more effective than any other sense in evoking associations and calling forth the past, often in vivid detail. This is true even though it is difficult to imagine odors clearly. We can see a face or hear a bell in imagination, and we know the smell of baking bread and scrambled eggs, but we cannot really revive them at will. Remembering what an odor smells like is not the same as actually smelling it, if only in imagination, and doesn't have the same effect. A whiff of perking coffee can bring back whole scenes of family breakfasts and frosty mornings, something that imagining coffee's odor could never do. The associations evoked by odors usually have more emotional contents than those evoked by other senses. If this weren't so, the perfume industry would go out of business.

Even when we cannot identify an odor, its effect can be profound. No amount of sniffing will tell us what it is that smells like fall or impending snow, but they are there and they color our behavior. Even strong odors are not so easily identified as are sights and sounds, perhaps because we are more accustomed to identifying objects by their appearance or their names rather than by their odors (Engen 1982).

CHAPTER 8

Texture

Texture is the most complex of food's physical characteristics, and along with flavor it is the quality that most frequently comes to mind when one thinks of specific food items (Szczesniak 1975). Yet it is rarely studied by psychologists, probably because experimentally controlled studies are difficult to carry out. Not only is there no single set of receptors responsible for the perception of texture, but also texture changes so rapidly when food is being eaten that measurements are difficult to take.

Definitions

Broadly defined, *texture* as a subjectively experienced quality refers to the feel of food in the mouth and the impression one has of its physical characteristics as a result of biting and chewing (Kramer 1973). (Visual texture is a matter of appearance.) There is a wide variety of words used to describe texture, depending on whether one is emphasizing the structure, consistency, or "mouthfeel" of the foods (Kramer 1973). One standard set of physical characteristics is shown in tables 8-1 and 8-2, which also show the comparable popular terms. Table 8-1 refers to solid or semisolid foods (Szczesniak 1963), and table 8-2 refers to liquids (Szczesniak 1979). If the texture concept is broadened, impressions of temperature, size, shape, spiciness, and astringency could be included.

Rheological Definitions

In spite of years of research, there is no fully accepted list of texture terms (Jowitt 1974). Some definitions, like those in tables 8-1 and 8-2, refer to the sensory or psychological properties of foods, while others refer to their rheological or engineering characteristics—the deformation and flow of matter. Many of the texture characteristics have been given technical or

TABLE **8-1.** **Relations between textural properties and popular nomenclature**

Mechanical characteristics

Primary parameters	Secondary parameters	Popular terms
Hardness		Soft → firm → hard
Cohesiveness	Fracturability	Crumbly → crunchy → brittle
	Chewiness	Tender → chewy → tough
	Gumminess	Short → mealy → pasty → gummy
Viscosity		Thin → viscous
Springiness		Plastic → elastic
Adhesiveness		Sticky → tacky → gooey

Geometrical characteristics

Class	Examples
Particle size and shape	Gritty, grainy, coarse, etc.
Particle shape and orientation	Fibrous, cellular, crystalline, etc.

Other characteristics

Primary parameters	Secondary parameters	Popular terms
Moisture content		Dry → moist → wet → watery
Fat content	Oiliness	Oily
	Greasiness	Greasy

Reprinted by permission from: Szczesniak, A. S. (1963). Classification of textural characteristics. *Journal of Food Science.* 28: 385–89. © Institute of Food Technologists.

operational definitions based on the procedures used to measure them (Szczesniak 1966). Hardness is "the force necessary to attain a given deformation" (usually on the first bite). Chewiness is "the energy required to masticate a solid food product to a state ready for swallowing." Cohesiveness is "the rate at which the material disintegrates under mechanical action" (or "the strength of internal bonds which make up the body of the product"). Adhesiveness is "the work necessary to overcome the attraction forces between the surface of the food and the surface of other materials with which the food comes into contact." These technical definitions are important in laboratory research, but the popular terms shown in tables 8-1 and 8-2 are more meaningful to laypeople and foodservice personnel.

Physiology of Texture Perception

Sensations of touch and pressure, temperature, pain, tissue dryness, salivary secretion, sound, and even tickle, alone or in combination, give

TABLE 8-2. **Classification of sensory mouthfeel terms for liquids**

Category	% total responses	typical words
I Viscosity-related terms	30.7	thin, thick, viscous
II Feel on soft tissue surfaces	17.6	smooth, pulpy, creamy
III Carbonation-related terms	11.2	bubbly, tingly, foamy
IV Body-related terms	10.2	heavy, watery, light
V Chemical effect	7.3	astringent, burning, sharp
VI Coating of oral cavity	4.5	mouthcoating, clinging, fatty, oily
VII Resistance to tongue movement	3.6	slimy, syrupy, pasty, sticky
VIII Afterfeel-mouth	2.2	clean, drying, lingering, cleansing
IX Afterfeel-physiological	3.7	refreshing, warming, thirst-quenching, filling
X Temperature-related	4.4	cold, hot
XI Wetness-related	1.3	wet, dry

Reprinted by permission from: Szczesniak, A. S. (1979). Classification of mouthfeel characteristics of beverages. In P. Sherman, ed., *Food texture and rheology*. New York: Academic Press.

rise to texture's many qualities. Unlike taste and smell, the perception of texture depends on activity in several different sensory systems, especially somasthesis (the skin senses) and kinesthesis and proprioception (the movement senses) in the muscles, tendons, and joints of the mouth and jaw (Kenshalo 1971). Hearing may also play a role in detecting qualities such as crispness or brittleness. Although kinesthesis and touch and pressure are the most important senses in texture perception, the senses usually work together and thus it is difficult to account for any given quality on the basis of a single specific sense.

Impressions of the geometrical characteristics, viscosity, and most of the liquid textures of food depend primarily on sensations of touch. Impressions of the mechanical characteristics require movement of the mouth and jaw and, with the possible exception of viscosity, depend on the amount of force or pressure required to fracture the food or change its shape. For gumminess, deformation pressure is most important, but for hardness, it is unclear whether rupture or deformation pressures give the better clues (Christensen 1984). It is also unclear whether subjective judgments of hardness are made on the basis of the first bite or on the amount of force needed to break down the food by subsequent chewing.

In spite of the importance of texture in food acceptance and enjoyment, most of the detailed information we have about the senses involved in texture perception is based on studies from parts of the body other than the mouth, gums, and jaw. Those studies use standard, highly artificial stimuli: warm and cold stylus points to study temperature sensitivity, for example, or single horsehairs of different diameters and bendability to study touch and pressure on the skin, or rubber disks of different thicknesses to study biting force (Woodworth and Schlosberg 1954). Normally, however, bits and pieces of food in the mouth vary in several dimensions or characteristics at the same time, and it would be impossible to isolate each of these without so altering the food that the study would be meaningless. Further, food is continually being modified by chewing and dilution with saliva, so it does not remain constant—a condition required for precise experimentation. Chewing also releases tastes and odors that may affect texture perception.

Kinesthesis: Muscles, Tendons, Joints

Biting and chewing activate pressure receptors deep in the gums as well as kinesthetic receptors in the muscles, tendons, and joints of the jaw. These receptors convey information regarding the amount of muscle contraction and jaw movement, and give impressions of the hardness, toughness, and chewiness of foods.

Touch and Pressure

In vision, taste, and smell the sensory experiences are correlated with activity in specific kinds of receptors. This is not always the case for the skin senses, although the different qualities do seem to have characteristic receptor-nerve fiber units (Christensen 1984; Matlin 1983; Woodworth and Schlosberg 1954). Generally, there are two kinds of skin, or somasthetic, receptor mechanisms: free nerve endings which function for pain, and encapsulated nerve endings with specific kinds of receptor cells (Wilentz 1968). Activation of some of those cells seems to be at least partially correlated with sensory qualities, for example, Kraus end bulbs with cold, Meissner corpuscles with light touch, and Pucinian corpuscles with deep touch or pressure. There is no consistent relation, however, between the kind of receptor activated and the quality or kind of sensation experienced. Cold can be felt if the skin is stimulated where there are no Kraus end bulbs and not be experienced where there are. It doesn't even require a cold object to produce a cold sensation. In paradoxical cold, cold is felt with a warm stimulus. Paradoxical warmth has also been reported, as when a frigid piece of metal feels momentarily hot to the touch. On some parts of the skin, a warm stimulus produces a complex of sensations including warmth, itch, prick, sting, and pain (Krech and Crutchfield 1958).

At present, it is not known whether the lack of consistent relations between receptors and sensory qualities is real or whether it only appears so because there is insufficient information due to the difficulty of carrying out research on the skin senses (Woodworth and Schlosberg 1954).

Touch sensations are produced by indentations of the skin or activation of receptors at the endings of hair follicles. In the mouth, receptors in the tongue, cheeks, throat, and gums are involved. As the force applied increases, pressure is experienced. Biting and chewing activate receptors deeper in the gums as well as kinesthetic receptors in the muscles, tendons, and joints of the jaw.

Touch sensitivity: Sensitivity to touch is different for different parts of the body. Under appropriate conditions we are able to detect indentations as small as 400 thousandths of an inch. The sole of the foot is about a hundred times less sensitive to pressure than the tip of the tongue, which is about 50 percent more sensitive than the fingertips (Woodworth and Schlosberg 1954). The gums are ten times more sensitive to pressure on the front teeth than on the back teeth. This allows the back teeth to do more chewing and grinding without discomfort. The extra sensitivity of the front teeth may also have a practical purpose of warning us not to try to ingest objects that are too hard to bite into.

Vibration and roughness: Successive indentation is called vibration and is the basis for the perception of roughness. As the fingers or tongue move over a coarse surface, the successive vibrations are less frequent than would be felt with a fine surface. The ear is much more sensitive to vibrations than is the skin. We can detect sound when the eardrum is displaced by only 0.000000001 of a centimeter; the eardrum is most sensitive to vibrations of 3,000 cycles per second. On the skin we cannot detect displacements smaller than 0.00001 of a centimeter; we are most sensitive to vibrations of 300 cycles per second (Matlin 1983).

Haptic perception: Active touch, called haptic perception, involves the identification of objects by manipulating and exploring them with our fingers or, in eating, with our mouth and tongue. There seems to be a slight loss with age in the ability to identify objects on the basis of touch (Kenshalo 1977). Kinesthetic feedback from the movement and position of the jaw is also important. From those various sensations, we are able to estimate the sizes and shapes of food particles and to identify other qualities as well.

In the mouth we are able to detect particles perhaps as small as twelve thousandths of a millimeter in diameter (Christensen 1984), thus the smallest grain of sand is noticeable. The difference threshold, or the amount by which a particle must be increased or decreased in size for us to notice the change, is approximately 10 percent.

Texture Measurement

Food texture has been measured in a variety of ways including adjective checklists and mechanical devices ranging from motorized dentures to complex instruments that simulate the movements of biting and chewing and record the time functions of the various forces at work (Bourne 1982).

Not at all   Very much so

Crisp	▢	▢	▢	▢	▢	▢
Soft	▢	▢	▢	▢	▢	▢
Airy	▢	▢	▢	▢	▢	▢
Brittle	▢	▢	▢	▢	▢	▢
Chunky	▢	▢	▢	▢	▢	▢
Flaky	▢	▢	▢	▢	▢	▢
Soggy	▢	▢	▢	▢	▢	▢
Dry	▢	▢	▢	▢	▢	▢
Bad	▢	▢	▢	▢	▢	▢
Chewy	▢	▢	▢	▢	▢	▢
Crunchy	▢	▢	▢	▢	▢	▢
Hard	▢	▢	▢	▢	▢	▢
Slippery	▢	▢	▢	▢	▢	▢
Doughy	▢	▢	▢	▢	▢	▢
Good	▢	▢	▢	▢	▢	▢
Gritty	▢	▢	▢	▢	▢	▢

8-1. Typical consumer texture profile ballot for cold cereals. (Reprinted with permission from Szczesniak, A. S., Leow, B. J., and Skinner, E. Z. (1975). Consumer texture profile technique. *Journal of Food Science*, 40: 1253–56. Copyright © by Institute of Food Technologists)

Subjective Evaluations

The Consumer Texture Profile Technique is a common method of evaluating food textures (Szczesniak et al. 1975). A list of adjectives describing the texture of a specific food is compiled by a panel of experts. The list is then modified to include some antonyms as well as terms indicating different intensities, such as *soft, firm, hard*. The texture of the food is then rated on a six-point scale ranging from "not at all" to "very much so" for each of the texture terms. Different terms are used for different foods, as appropriate. It is also possible to specify an ideal profile for a given food and to compare individual samples with it. A profile "ballot" for cold cereals is shown in figure 8-1. The technique has the advantage that the terms are easily understood and the descriptive profile is meaningful to laypeople as well as to professionals.

Mechanical Measurements

Three classes of tests have been used in the instrumental measurement of food texture: *fundamental* tests, *empirical* tests, and *imitative* tests (Bourne 1978).

Fundamental tests measure physical properties of foods—such as strength, shear, and bulk. Such measures are characteristic of engineering analyses and do not correlate very well with subjective evaluations of texture.

Empirical tests separately measure a variety of characteristics that are important in texture quality. Among them are shear, extrusion, and resistance to puncture. Some of the tests give results that correlate fairly well with subjective evaluations of texture for specific food items.

Imitative tests use instruments to imitate cutting, forking, or spooning or, more usually, the conditions of biting and chewing that food undergoes from service to swallowing. Two major instruments, both of which have been used successfully, are the Instron Universal Testing Machine and the General Foods Texturometer (Bourne 1982). The techniques are known as "texture profile analyses," and the measurements are often presented as "force-time curves." Analysis of curves from the Texturometer led to the identification of seven basic texture dimensions or characteristics (Szczesniak 1975), some of which were defined above. Five of the characteristics are directly measured: fracturability, hardness, cohesiveness, adhesiveness, and springiness or elasticity. Two are calculated from other measures: gumminess, which is the product of hardness and cohesiveness; and chewiness, which is the product of hardness, cohesiveness, and springiness (Bourne 1982). These characteristics are technically important, but they have less practical everyday value in foodservice and enjoyment than do subjective qualities and evaluations. Nor are they particularly helpful in food preparation because they are not basic in the same sense that odors or tastes can be basic.

The Modification of Texture
Salivation

Texture changes in the mouth are brought about by salivation, biting, and chewing. Saliva is secreted by three major pairs of glands: the parotid, which are located in the cheek walls opposite the upper molars, and the submaxillary and sublingual, which are located on the floor of the mouth opposite the base of the front part of the tongue (Christensen 1984). Mucus which lubricates and binds the food particles together also is secreted. The amount of saliva secreted at any time depends on individual differences, one's emotional state, and the specific food being eaten. The amount can vary by as much as eight times, even among healthy individuals, and differences in customary mouth dryness may have some effect on food preferences. Emotions such as fear reduce the flow of saliva. This knowledge was used in a primitive lie-detection test in which the suspect was given dry rice to swallow. In theory, if the person was guilty, his mouth would become so dry from fear that he would not be able to swallow the rice and thus he would reveal his guilt (Woodworth and Schlosberg 1954). Acid foods are the most effective in increasing the flow of saliva, but the flow can be increased by any substance producing sensations of irritation. The sight, smell, or thought of food can also have that effect; it occurs commonly in the presence of foods containing sour or pungent ingredients (Christensen and Navazesh 1984).

Saliva is 99 percent water, but it also contains ptyalin, an enzyme for the digestion of starches (Christensen 1984; Williams 1974). The liquid softens the food, assists in its breakdown, and makes swallowing easier. When mixed with food by chewing, saliva helps release and dissolve chemicals important in odors and tastes. Thus it plays a role in both texture and flavor perception.

Chewing

Chewing gives impressions of food's texture qualities even while it is changing those qualities and making the food ready for swallowing and digestion. During chewing, the upper jaw is stationary while the lower jaw moves in opening, closing, sidewise, and protrusive movements (Christensen 1984). After the first bite, the movement follows a figure-eight pattern and is usually on one side only, although the food may be shifted from one side to another during chewing. The pattern varies somewhat for different foods. For example, the movement is more vertical and chopping for hard, crisp foods like carrots but more lateral and grinding for tough, chewy foods. Pressures of up to 5 pounds are applied on the incisors and up to 200 pounds on the molars where most chewing takes place (Williams 1974). The rate of chewing is slower at first. It is unclear whether the rate is faster or slower for hard foods (Christensen 1984), but the number of strokes per minute before swallowing does vary with hardness. One study reported an average rate of zero for water, 11.5 for mashed potatoes, and 103 for hard candy (Pierson and LeMagnen 1970). Large particles also are chewed more rapidly than smaller ones (Yurkstas 1965).

There are individual differences in chewing patterns, including the teeth used, the speed, and the size to which the food is reduced before swallowing. These are due to tooth patterns and sensitivity of the teeth and gums as well as to individual differences in acquired chewing habits.

Texture Mixtures

Odors tend to fuse or blend when combined, but textures, like taste qualities, do not. They combine as mixtures in which the separate textures remain discernible. Texture combinations add interest to food, but not all are desirable. We do not like lumpy pudding, gravy or mashed potatoes, or bits of anything in liquids. Pieces of walnut or chocolate chips in cookies are all right. So are pieces of pistachio in ice cream or bits of onion in mashed potatoes. Bits of softer texture in hard foods are often enjoyable. Bits of harder texture in soft foods can be unacceptable if they are unexpected, but that depends on the foods. However, if those harder textures are lumps of the same food, they seem always to be unacceptable. For example, many people like chopped peanuts in soft peanut butter, but would not like soft peanut butter containing harder lumps of peanut butter.

Adaptation

Adaptation to touch and pressure occurs very rapidly (Matlin 1983). On the forearm, pressure sensitivity is 20 percent of its initial value after three and a half seconds, and we barely notice the weight of clothes after we put them on. Adaptation to food in the mouth might occur rapidly, but the food is constantly in motion so adaptation that requires continuous stimulation of the same receptor areas is minimized.

The Effect of Texture on Flavor

Texture, like appearance, taste, and smell, can alter the perceived flavor of food. When hard ice cream is softened, it feels and "tastes" creamier and more delicate. Producers of soft ice cream take advantage of this and are able to market ice milk, which tastes rich and creamy when soft but watery and flavorless when hard. The semifluid texture and slightly warmer temperature also release flavorings, and the ice milk seems more full-bodied. Perhaps this is why ice milk is usually available only in vanilla. Other flavorings might interfere with the subtle tastes and detract from the enjoyment of the texture.

The introduction of imitation foods, such as margarine and imitation bacon and crabmeat, requires the judicious use of texture for the imitation to be acceptable. "Soft" margarine seems more like butter than regular margarine does because of its lower melting point and softer feel in the mouth. Bacon substitutes smell and taste like bacon and more or less look like it, but they don't have bacon's texture. They are tough and chewy and therefore they don't "taste" the same. Imitation crabmeat, on the other hand, has had better acceptance. Besides being made to look and smell like crab and to have the sweetish taste of crab—qualities that are difficult to duplicate—it has been processed to *feel* like crabmeat as well, with a slightly chewy stringiness. The texture makes the difference between a good and a mediocre imitation.

Texture Meanings

Appearance and aroma can be experienced independently of eating, and therefore they can become associated with any part of the broad context in which they occur. We can smell bakery goods while we are still in the street, and their odor may bring back memories of specific times and places. Since we cannot experience food texture unless food is actually in our mouths, texture is less likely to evoke thoughts of foods other than the one we are eating and less likely to develop the kinds of associations that occur with appearance and aroma. In this respect, texture is similar to taste. The sight of carrots or green beans can remind us of a childhood garden, but it is doubtful that their sweetness or chewy crispness would. Impressions of texture based on touching or feeling the food with our fingers or hands are even less likely to do so.

On the other hand, the poor ability of textures to evoke associations is more than made up for by the variety and strength of the meanings they

TABLE 8-3. **Connotative meanings of various texture terms**

Term	Meaning
Crispness	The most versatile texture; universally liked; not satiating; synonymous with freshness and wholesomeness.
Tenderness	Indicates quality and good nutrition; preferred in meat and some young vegetables.
Crumbliness	Usually an aesthetically undesirable characteristic.
Juiciness	Well liked; appetizing and appealing; suggests satiating and nourishing qualities.
Sponginess	Associated with dainty foods, usually desserts.
Sogginess	Suggests staleness or poor preparation.
Gumminess	Unpleasant when occurring with rubbery, tough or stringy qualities; pleasant with creaminess, softness, or stickiness in desserts.
Firmness	One of the most positive textures; considered ideal for many foods.
Crunchiness	Associated with well-liked, wholesome, and nourishing "fun" foods; active, energetic, and appealing.
Mealiness	Usually a negative quality with low interest and appeal.
Hardness	Except for a few foods, it is negative and implies an unappetizing quality. Acceptable when transitory.
Softness	A passive texture, but widely liked except in excess; may be considered childish and weak.

Adapted from Szczesniak, A. S. and Kahn, E. L. (1971). Consumer awareness of and attitudes to food texture. *Journal of Texture Studies*, 2: 280–95.

convey. Some of these are shown in table 8-3 (Szczesniak and Kahn 1971). Some textures, such as firmness in fruits and vegetables, identify food qualities, but others have much broader connotations. Juiciness, crispness, and tenderness convey wholesomeness and good nutrition but are less likely to mean that the food is substantial and filling. This has implications for menu planning and food acceptance. We may *know* that fruits and vegetables are good for us, but they don't make us *feel* that they are because they are not particularly filling.

Texture and Food Preferences

As with tastes and odors, there are only a few universally liked or disliked food textures. Most texture preferences depend on the food in question and secondarily on individual differences. No one likes limp toast, but some like it crisp throughout while others like it soft inside.

Rubbery foods are generally disliked, especially if chewing does not alter the shape. Poorly cooked octopus or overly thick gelatin can be bitten and temporarily transformed, but when the pressure is removed they return to their original shape. Elastic foods such as tough meat change their shape when chewed but do not fragment or separate into smaller pieces. Some elasticity is acceptable and adds interest but, even in chewing gum, it is not satisfying for long or by itself and needs the extraction of flavor to make it desirable.

"Slimy" and "slippery" are not positive adjectives whether referring to food or people, and there is a general aversion to slimy foods or at least to their feel in the mouth; even those who like raw oysters swallow them quickly. There are a few regional preferences such as boiled okra, which is somewhat slimy, but liking probably does not depend on the okra's texture. Among individuals there are also differences in preferences and sensitivity. Some people find ripe persimmons too slimy to be appetizing. For others the sliminess is not noticed or is outweighed by the flavor. When tough or slimy foods are liked it is usually *in spite of* their textures, but when they are disliked it is usually *because of* their textures.

The most general positive texture preference is for solid foods that are somewhat soft but require some biting and chewing, but the preference is highly dependent on the particular food. Softness and smoothness are widely preferred in desserts, but not in meats. (Those who like liver probably do so in spite of its softness.) Custards should be very soft; meat should be tender; cooked vegetables should be firm, and salad vegetables should be crisp.

Texture preferences also vary with the emotions being experienced, as discussed in chapter 4, although the preferences may be a function of the kinds of foods preferred as well as of the textures.

It is interesting that while several of the negative textures are disliked in any food, none of the positive ones is always liked. It is also interesting that there are many more negative texture terms than positive ones. This parallels the fact that there are more negative than positive emotions and fits the suggestion made elsewhere that different dynamics are involved in liking and disliking or in pleasantness and unpleasantness, and that they are not simply extremes of the same continuum. This is also confirmed by the fact that specific identifiable physical characteristics, including textures, are more often mentioned when food is disliked than when it is liked. In the latter, other kinds of associations seem more important. The relation between associations and food preferences is discussed more fully in chapter 11.

Texture and Menu-Category Preferences

In specific menu categories the preference for texture qualities is much less clear than it is with odor qualities. Some preferences depend on texture meanings such as those shown in table 8-3, but as suggested earlier, most depend on the particular food item. We prefer a limited variety of textures at breakfast and prefer the greatest variety at dinner (Szczesniak and Kahn 1971). Generally, chewiness is more preferred in meats but not in main dishes such as fish or casseroles. Heaviness emphasizes a food and is most liked when it coincides with the main meal item. Lightness is liked in salads and desserts. Soups should be neither too thin nor too thick, with more thickness acceptable if the soup is made from solid, heavy foods. Split-pea or bean soup seems right if it is thicker than tomato soup. Crispness is appropriate for salads, vegetables, and some desserts, but softness is more likely to be preferred in the latter.

In menu planning, variety and balance are important. Variety and contrast add interest and taste appeal. Balance is aesthetically pleasing when the textures used fit the particular food as well as the relative importance of that food in the meal as a whole. The senses interact not only among themselves but also with meanings; thus, relationships are important. No doubt there is a fittingness of texture, tastes, odors, and appearances which skilled chefs and menu planners know intuitively, but which have not yet been identified by psychologists.

CHAPTER 9

Appearance

Appearance, flavor, and texture are the major determiners of food acceptance and the guiding trilogy in food preparation and service. What food looks like influences not only what foods we select when a variety is offered but also can affect the taste of foods and our enjoyment of them. It is the most important factor in supermarket displays. Many varieties of fruits and vegetables that excelled in flavor but were undistinguished in appearance have been replaced by the big, the bright, and the beautiful because that is what customers want. The nondescript-looking George IV peach and the Seckel pear are not available although they are superb in flavor. Smaller, more flavorful strains of carrots, blueberries, strawberries, and the like are ignored in favor of larger, more colorful ones.

The effects of texture and flavor depend on relatively direct contact with food, but appearance operates at a distance. In cafeterias, bakeries, and self-serve restaurants appearance guides our choices and establishes a set of expectations for flavor even before the food is tasted.

Appearance and Presentation

Carême, the great French chef, gave the highest priority to appearance or presentation. The making of sweets he considered to be a branch of architecture: "The fine arts are five in number, to wit: painting, sculpture, poetry, music, architecture—whose main branch is confectionary" (Montagne 1961). This view guided him in the preparation and presentation of other foods as well. He was an expert in the execution of *pièces montées*, decorative pieces whose particular function was to "excite the appetite." He believed all cooking should be decorative and made detailed drawings for a wide variety of dishes. He created, or perhaps more correctly, *constructed* masterpieces of design and style.

97

Garnishes

Elaborate presentations are no longer in vogue, although one sometimes sees vestiges of the old style in elegant buffets with ice carvings and intricately prepared foods. Appearance, however, is still extremely important in food acceptance and satisfaction, and there is an increasing awareness of its importance. The simple sprig of parsley is no longer enough to make a dish attractive. There is renewed interest in the garnishes of French cuisine which, contrary to popular assumption, were meant to be eaten. Usually they are vegetables but they may be made of almost any food. Simple garnishes consist of a single item, and composite garnishes are made from several ingredients. Traditionally, garnishes are placed around offerings of meat, fish, or poultry; or they may be served on a separate dish as an accompaniment. Their flavor should always blend with the basic dish, and they should be decorative as well in order to add to the appearance and enjoyment of the food.

Visual Perception

Visual perception depends on the transmission of light waves, reflected through the lens of the eye from objects in the environment and projected onto the retina where they activate specialized receptor cells. The receptors for color are known as cones, and those for black and white and dim illumination are known as rods. From the retina, nerve impulses are transmitted along fibers of the optic nerve to the visual areas of the cortex of the brain.

Characteristics of Perception

Organization: One of the basic facts of visual perception is that it is organized. We do not see isolated bits and pieces of objects and from those create the object. Rather, we perceive objects as wholes, even when only a part of the object actually is seen. The perception of a tree is not a collection of branches added together to form a tree, although their shape and color contribute to the perception. Nor is it necessary to see the whole tree or all of its branches in order to have a clear impression of it.

Figure-ground relations: Objects also stand out from their backgrounds and have meaning. This is known as the figure-ground relation. The word *figure* should not be taken too literally. It refers to anything on which attention is focused. As you read this line, the sentence is figure and the page is background. As you look at a table set for dinner, the table is figure and the whole room is background, but if attention is focused on the flowers or on a plate, the rest of the table is background.

The figure-ground relation is shown in the reversible figure (fig. 9-1). When attention is focused on one part, a vase is seen and the rest is background, but a shift of attention makes the vase background for the two

9–1. Reversible figure

profiles facing each other. The figure, whether vase or profiles, has definite shape and meaning while backgrounds do not. The figure is bounded and limited. The background is unbounded. It extends beneath and behind the figure and seems to continue beyond the actual visual field, including the unseen world behind the viewer.

Fluctuations of attention: The reversible figure demonstrates another fact of perception: attention fluctuates. As you continue to look at the drawing, the figures shift so that one form is seen and then the other. The vase and profiles shift back and forth even if we try to prevent this, and what is seen changes even though there is no change in what is presented. In the everyday world there are few situations involving reversible figures, but attention shifts spontaneously nevertheless, and it is impossible to prevent those shifts.

The reversible figure also demonstrates that it is not possible to pay full attention to more than one thing at a time. We see either the vase or the profiles. We cannot see both at once. In the complex world, too, only one thing can be dominant in attention. All else is either unseen or is seen only peripherally.

There are also shifts of attention because of eye movements known as saccades. The eye is constantly in motion darting from one fixation point to another. The movements occur irregularly at an average rate of about two to four per second, with fixations of about one-fifth of a second unless attention is also focused (Murch 1973). Although the movements can be controlled, they occur spontaneously, and even when we look at an object, saccadic movements continue to occur with fixations on different parts of the object. These eye movements give us information about the object and also help us to be aware of the many different objects in our environment. They are especially important in driving, for example, where they keep us informed of the ever-changing scene by bringing objects from peripheral vision into clear focus. They are also extremely important in the perception of stationary objects. They give us detail and information about size and shape which help tell us what an object is.

Span of apprehension: Just as the attention span is limited, so is the span of apprehension, or the number of items that can be seen correctly at a glance. The usual estimate is seven plus or minus two (Miller 1956). Beyond that, we guess; or, with longer periods of fixation, we can count the items.

Closure and set: Because the eye moves from fixation point to fixation point rather than tracing or covering all parts of an object, we do not actually see an object so much as form impressions of it. This tendency is enhanced by fluctuations of attention and the span of apprehension. The information taken in by the eye is combined into a coherent whole, partly by the phenomenon of closure and partly by set or expectation. In *closure*, missing bits and pieces are filled in or not noticed as missing. For example, in reading a sentence an "a" or "the" can often be omitted, but we can read the sentence several times without noticing the omission. Similarly, when we see a person moving by a window, we have the impression of a whole person walking by even though we see only the head and torso. *Set*, or *expectation*, supplies "missing" parts and influences what we perceive.

Sets and expectations also affect how we perceive ambiguous or unclear stimuli. Most objects are ambiguous because we actually see only parts of them, and, therefore, sets and expectations are especially important in perception. Even when the whole object is present, we tend to see what we expect to see unless the object is quite clear or we pay close attention to it.

Implications for Foodservice

The facts of eye movements, fluctuations of attention, and the span of apprehension suggest considerations for foodservice. First, since most perceptions are impressions, decor, service, and the social and physical atmosphere become important because they establish sets and expectations that influence the way in which specific foods are perceived as well as the meanings attributed to those foods.

Second, there should be interest and variety in setting and service so that the eye can move and attention can shift from one interest point to another and yet keep returning to some central part for which all else is enhancing context. It is important that the setting and the way materials are presented accomplish this goal. In table service, as elsewhere, clutter creates confusion, but too much simplicity creates disinterest and boredom unless it is carefully carried out. Attention is attracted by the physically dominant object and by unusual forms, bright colors, pleasing combinations, and unexpected contrasts. If two or more items are equally important, attention will be divided among them and there will be no central focus of interest. Elaborate crystal out of keeping with the food being served or the rest of the setting overemphasizes wine and water and detracts from the food itself, making it seem dull and insignificant.

Shape

It would seem reasonable to suppose that the perception of form or shape should depend on the pattern of light projected on the retina, just as a photograph of an object depends on the projection of light through the camera lens onto the film. But the eye is not a camera. It does not work that way, and much about the perception of form remains unknown. One of the most interesting facts is that contour or outline alone does not determine shape. In the moon-face example shown in figure 9-2, there is a single center line, so the contour is the same regardless of which profile is seen. Yet the same contour gives two radically different profiles. The one facing right has a sharp nose and prominent lips; the one facing left has a rounded nose and a prominent chin. The difference in profiles is due in part to the fact that the facial contour is seen as belonging to the left or right arcs of the circle and to enclose different spaces depending on where attention is focused. The reversible figure cited earlier also demonstrates that contour alone does not determine shape. The same contours form a vase at one time and two profiles at another.

Basic Shapes

Artists say that there are four basic shapes—cube, cone, cylinder, and sphere—out of which all others can be constructed. Simple objects may consist of only one of these, while complex ones are a combination of two or more. In ice sculpture, for example, the cube is the basis of a boat, house, castle, tray; a cone makes a tree, vase, candle flame, fish; a cylinder makes a candle, body, arm, leg; and a sphere makes a bowl, vase, head (Amendola 1969). Psychologists studying visual perception have not identified basic shapes, unless curves, angles, and straight lines qualify as such. Probably this is because perception research has dealt almost exclusively with two-dimensional drawings rather than with three-dimensional objects of the real world.

9–2. Moon faces

Shape Constancy

When the image of an object is projected through the lens of the eye onto the retina, the retinal image corresponds in shape to the pattern of light waves reflected from the object. Thus, the retinal image of a plate is always elliptical unless the plate is viewed full face. Nevertheless, the plate *looks* round regardless of the angle from which it is viewed. This is known as *shape constancy*. The reasons for it are not entirely understood, but it almost always occurs unless illumination is very poor, even if the actual shape of the object is unknown.

Form and Meaning

Psychologists have not been particularly interested in the psychological significance of shapes. This is surprising, since humans have always been fascinated with forms and have given them a variety of meanings, as the recent craze for pyramids and Rubik's Cube suggests. The ancient Greeks thought the sphere was the perfect form, and in the 1600s the philosopher Descartes believed the seat of the soul was in the pineal gland, partly because it is spherical in shape and therefore a suitable housing for something eternal and divine. In heraldry, Druidic thought, and a number of cultures, the ring or annulet represents eternity. Crystals are thought by some to have healing powers, and the ancient Egyptians believed that pyramids transmitted cosmic energy.

In contemporary times, Freudian psychoanalysts have emphasized the sexual symbolism of elongated and roundish shapes, but systematic studies have been limited to a few investigations of the meaning and emotional values of lines or simple line drawings.

In one study, lines with angles, intersections, and irregular changes in direction were found to express ugliness and unpleasantness while those with an absence of angles and intersections expressed beauty and pleasantness (Lundholm 1921). Designs with curved lines represent quiet, soft emotions, and those with angles represent rougher, more vigorous ones (Hevner 1935). Table 9-1 shows the results when sixty college students were asked which of the nonsense forms, A or B, in figure 9-3, better represented each concept in table 9-1. All the differences, except for behavior, elation, psychology, and status, were statistically significant (Lyman 1979).

Form and Meaning in Foods

In the absence of information detailing the meanings of three-dimensional forms, the relation between form and meaning in foods must rely on generalizations from other areas. The studies above suggest that foods having irregular, jagged shapes might carry stronger, somewhat unpleas-

TABLE **9-1. Percent of individuals indicating whether Form A or B best represented each concept (Total N = 60)***

Concept	Figure A	Figure B	Concept	Figure A	Figure B
1. amused	92	8	21. hostile	5	95
2. anxious	5	95	22. jealous	13	87
3. angry	0	100	23. kind	98	2
4. behavior	43	57	24. love	92	8
5. bored	65	35	25. maluma	93	7
6. brave	20	80	26. mature	80	20
7. calm	100	0	27. music	75	25
8. consciousness	20	80	28. needed	90	10
9. country	82	18	29. nervous	5	95
10. dull	95	5	30. philosophy	34	66
11. elation	62	38	31. psychology	50	50
12. embarrassed	28	72	32. resentful	0	100
13. eternity	87	13	33. sad	87	13
14. excited	12	88	34. self	88	12
15. fearful	3	97	35. self-confident	80	20
16. friendly	98	2	36. solemn	29	71
17. frustrated	5	95	37. status	58	42
18. good	98	2	38. takete	12	88
19. happy	90	10	39. wise	87	13
20. home	92	8	40. worried	13	87

*N = 59 for consciousness, philosophy, solemn, status.

Reprinted by permission from: Lyman, B. (1979). Representation of complex emotional and abstract meanings by simple forms. *Perceptual and Motor Skills, 49:* 839–42.

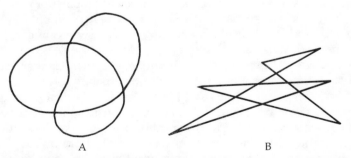

A   B

ant meanings, while smooth, rounded foods carry calmer, more pleasant ones. To some extent this may be true, but the inference must be tempered by the fact that smooth, rounded forms in foods prepared for eating often occur in ones that are bland and undistinguished in flavor or texture, such as molded puddings and gelatins, or in ones in which the shape has been artificially contrived. Irregularly shaped food servings are more natural.

Natural Forms and Shapes

In pleasant emotions, images of nature and naturally occurring objects and scenes are much more frequent than images of manmade ones (Lyman and Waters, in press). This suggests that natural, uncontrived shapes in foods will be more pleasant. The scoop of mashed potatoes served in restaurants is less appealing than a serving with less symmetry and less suggestion of mass production. With ice cream, a scoop is fine because it is a manufactured food, but uneven spoonfuls might better convey a home-made feeling. Complex, unnatural forms are more likely to be pleasing for special effects, especially when one wants to make the point that great care and effort went into preparing the food. An egg cooked in a poacher has a perfect circular form, but it seems less appetizing than one with a more natural shape, partly because the latter is natural and partly because the less perfect circle is actually more difficult to attain. Intricate hors d'oeuvres or a perfect dome of chocolate mousse is attractive not only because of color and form but also because the complexity of the one and the simplicity of the other suggest a caring concern in their preparation.

With the exception of meats, most food items that are not mixtures or combined with other foods are more appealing when their natural shapes are retained. Melon balls preserve the melon shape; melon cubes do not. Vegetables are sometimes cubed but almost never when served raw and rarely when they are cooked unless they are in soups or combined with something else. With meat, we seem to prefer the natural shape disguised, perhaps because of some deep-seated aversion to eating parts of what were once living creatures. Tongue is sometimes served *au naturel,* but not to the delight of many, and whole calf's brains, no matter how nicely garnished, would have no appeal at all.

Fish and poultry are exceptions to the general principle: their natural shapes are sometimes enhanced in preparation, usually on more formal occasions. For Americans, whole roast turkey has festive meanings as well as connotations of comfort, security, and ancestral triumph over adversity. Perhaps some unconscious hint of the hunt or the catch condones the use of squab, pheasant, whole fish, or even suckling pig, but nowadays these are served in ways to enhance appearance and to heighten the impression of meticulous care in their preparation, almost as if to distract one's attention from the thought that the object once had life.

Size

The apparent size of an object depends partly on the size of the image the object projects onto the retina. The larger the object, the larger the retinal image. When two objects are of equal size, the closer one projects the larger image. As an observer moves away from an object or as the object moves from the observer, the retinal image becomes smaller; it becomes larger under reverse conditions.

Size Constancy

If perceived size depended solely on the size of the retinal image, a person would appear to shrink as he or she moved away from us, and a house at a distance would look like a dollhouse. Obviously that does not happen. Somehow the perceptual system takes into account the change in distance, and the perceived size of the object remains the same (Rock 1975). This is known as *size constancy*. If, for some reason, there is a breakdown in the cues to distance, the perceived size of the object becomes distorted. This is what happens in the well-known moon illusion. The full moon looks much smaller overhead than when rising on the horizon. The retinal size is the same in both locations, but because there are no cues to distance overhead, the visual system judges the overhead moon to be closer and compensates for this by making it look smaller than the horizon moon which is "computed" to be farther away (Rock 1975). The illusion is compounded further by the fact that since the horizon moon now seems larger it also seems closer.

Perception is Relational

The relation between distance and retinal size and perceived size has little bearing on the perceived size of near objects such as servings of food, but it does point out that much of perception is relational and often involves automatic, nonconscious comparisons that give distorted impressions of size. This is one of the reasons for the effects of context. Objects can be altered in appearance by their physical contexts or settings so that identical objects will look different and different objects will look the same. In the Muller-Lyer illusion in figure 3-1, lines of equal length are made to look unequal by placing a context of arrow heads at the ends of one line and arrow tails at the ends of the other. The line with the arrow tails looks longer. Lines that are somewhat unequal in length can be made to look equal by putting arrow heads on the longer line.

In the Hering illusion in figure 3-1, parallel lines appear bowed when presented in the context of lines radiating outward from a point between the parallel lines. Circles of identical hues can be made to look different by placing them on appropriately colored backgrounds, and circles of different hues will appear to be the same when appropriate backgrounds are used.

Illusions of Size and Shape

In figure 9-4, each pair of center circles in C, D, and F is the same size; so are the circles in E, one of which looks like a slice of kiwi fruit. The arches in A are also the same size; all straight lines in G are the same length; and the bottom line of the lower figure in B is the same length as the top line in

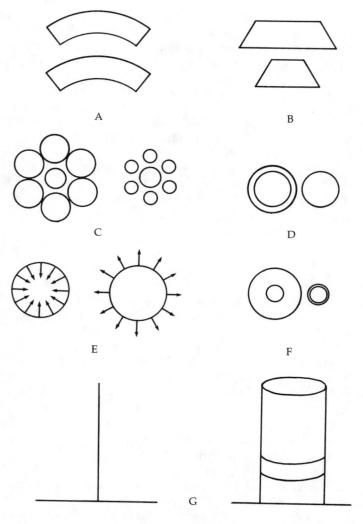

9–4. Optical illusions

the upper figure. In foodservice, the circle illusions show that portions will look larger if surrounded by a small garnish or served on a small plate. When reducing the size of servings, restaurants can maintain the illusion of no change by reducing the size of the serving plates or bowls. Children (and adults) will think they are getting a small portion of a disliked food if it is served in a large dish, and a larger portion of a forbidden food if it is served in a smaller dish. The arcs and horizontal-vertical illusions suggest that the perceived size of an individual food item can be affected by its position in relation to other foods on the same plate.

Emotions and Perceived Size

Emotions also can affect perceived size. Objects evoking pleasant or unpleasant emotions and objects with high value or need are estimated to be larger than neutral or meaningless objects. In a classic study, poor children overestimated the size of coins more than wealthy children did (Bruner and Goodman 1947). In another study, the size of coins was estimated to be larger than metal disks of the same size, and more valuable coins were overestimated more than less valuable ones (Baker et al. 1974). Chocolate bars were estimated to be larger than unpainted pieces of wood of the same size; and children estimated jars filled with candy to weigh more than jars filled with an equal weight of sand and sawdust (Dukes and Bevan 1952). In a familiar classroom demonstration, children are asked to draw a friendly, likable dog and an unfriendly ferocious one. Invariably the ferocious dog is drawn larger. Perhaps to the child, a small serving of hated vegetables actually does look larger than it is!

Size and Meaning

Bigger is not always better, but it is usually more important. In addition, larger objects attract attention unless the smaller ones are set off by contrast. Since the main dish, or entree, is the most important part of an American dinner, it should be the largest physically or be served so as to give that impression. In Chinese meals, where there is no central dish, servings are of equal size. A large salad served with a few cold cuts on the same plate is appropriate, but if a large salad is served with a small cutlet, the wrong item is emphasized. For the same reason, it is a violation of emphasis and aesthetics to have a large scoop of ice cream with a small slice of pie or to have the serving portion of vegetables outbalance the main dish they accompany. In order to achieve proper emphasis, slices of breakfast toast that are larger than the eggs they accompany are either cut and placed to the side around the eggs or are served on a separate, smaller plate.

Smallness also conveys meaning. According to custom, it means a sample and is used that way in appetizers to suggest the tone of what is to come. It is also equated with being rare, valuable, and costly, a meaning that is enhanced by an appropriate setting. A cluttered jewelry-store window has an air of cheapness about it in contrast to a window displaying a solitary ring or bracelet on a field of velvet. This kind of nonverbal communication is used in advertising and in foodservice as well. Thus, a single small petit four or French pastry is served on a large plate in order to convey an idea of special elegance in form and flavor. Of course, the size of any serving should be appropriate to the setting, the physical characteristics of the food, the relation of the food to the other foods being served, and the meanings and significance one wishes the serving to express.

CHAPTER 10
Color

Color is a nontechnical term that includes three different qualities or characteristics: hue, saturation, and brightness. These are interdependent, and a change in one quality usually produces changes in the others. Therefore, the terminology can become confusing. Everyday language is also ambiguous. "Dark" sometimes means dull, but it can also mean rich and vivid.

Color Qualities
Hue

Hue refers to what we mean by color—red, blue, green, and so on—the colors of the everyday world. Hue is the quality that distinguishes one color from all others in the color spectrum, as seen in a rainbow. These colors range from red through violet in the familiar Roy G Biv acronym (*red, orange, yellow, green, blue, indigo, violet*). Differences in perceived color depend on the length of light waves, measured in nanometers (millimicrons) or millionths of a millimeter, reflected from objects in the physical world. The visible range for humans is from approximately 400 nanometers for violet to 700 nanometers for red. Unseen ultraviolet, X, gamma, and cosmic rays are shorter than 400 nanometers. Beyond the red end of the visible spectrum are infrared, micro, TV, and radio waves (Gleitman 1981). Activity in the receptor cells and beyond may be more important than differences in light waves, since colors can be produced sometimes by slowly rotating a black and white disk or by projecting a filtered yellow onto a screen through black and white transparencies (Murch 1976), a process developed by E. H. Land, the inventor of the Polaroid Land Camera. The light waves activate color vision receptors in the eye, known as cones. As for all vision, nerve impulses are transmitted along the optic nerve to the visual areas of the cortex.

Saturation

Saturation refers to the purity or "strength" of color. Roughly, it is the amount of color present. Desaturation refers to the extent to which the color approaches a neutral or medium gray. A pure saturated color contains no gray. A dull gray-green sweater is low in saturation, but a rich, full green is high. Saturation is correlated with the complexity of light waves. A dull green sweater reflects light waves containing those for green but also some that combine to produce gray. In everyday language, a saturated color is clear, bright, and vivid. Desaturated colors have less color. If purity only is involved, desaturation could be thought of as the addition of medium gray until the color itself becomes a neutral gray. Colors desaturated in this way could be described as grayish pale colors.

Brightness

The third color quality is *brightness,* a term that is technically correct but confusing because it refers not to color intensity, which is what we usually mean by brightness, but to the amount of light present, with black being the absence of light. Sometimes brightness is equated with lightness. Brightness is a function of the amplitude of light waves. Light pink is a light or "bright" red and has the same hue as red. As pink becomes less bright, technically it becomes more red, which seems to be a contradiction in meaning. A rose pink is less bright than light pink, and a dusty rose-pink is also less saturated. Rather than thinking of brightness as the amount of light present, it is more useful to think of pigment colors and to describe those to which white has been added as light or pale clear colors and those to which black has been added as dark, dull colors.

Color Sensitivity

Usually color qualities function interactively; a change in one tends to go with changes in another, and any change is thought of as a change in color.

In general, one hue can be distinguished from another if the wavelengths differ by approximately 1 to 3 nanometers, being smallest in the middle, or yellow-orange to green-blue, part of the spectrum (Mueller 1965). When differences in color purity or saturation and brightness are included, the average person can distinguish as many as 350,000 different colors, and a trained observer can distinguish as many as 10 million (Judd and Kelly 1939). Yet there are fewer than 5,000 technical color terms (Bartley 1958); there are fewer than twenty-five color names in common usage; and across cultures, no language has more than eleven basic color terms (Dember and Warm 1979). (The Maori of New Zealand are reported to have had 3,000 color names, not because they used that many colors, but because the same color on a different object was given a different name [Merleau-Ponty 1962]). The number of basic color terms—that is, those used to refer *only* to colors and excluding terms such as rust or wine—ranges from two to eleven in various cultures (Rosch 1977). Since we can distinguish many more colors than we have names for, we may choose or reject one object over another on the basis of color even though we cannot give reasons by naming the colors.

Changes in Color
Color Mixing

Although different hues may be produced by pure light waves, they are more commonly produced by mixtures of reflected light waves. In mixing colored pigments, the light waves for all colors except the one we see are absorbed by the pigments, and for that reason the mixing of pigments is known as *subtractive color mixture.* The pigment primaries out of which all other colors, except white, can be produced are red, blue, and yellow. In *additive color mixture* colored lights are mixed. The light primaries from which almost all colors except brown can be produced are red, blue, and green. Yellow is a mixture of red and green lights; white is a mixture of all light waves; and black is the absence of light. Additive color mixing is used in stage lighting, and it has been used by artists, most notably the pointillist Seurat, who juxtaposed dots of pure color so that the reflected light would mix and give purer colors than those produced by mixing pigments.

Adaptation

When we look at a colored object for a period of time, the color becomes less bright and seems somewhat washed out. The effect is especially noticeable if we try to match the color we have been looking at to a blotch of the same color. This is an adaptation effect similar to that in the perception of odor, except that the effect is much weaker with colors, and a color never seems to disappear.

Negative Afterimages

Another color change occurs with what is known as the *negative after image.* As colored lights, some colors when mixed in proper proportions will produce a neutral gray. These are known as complementary colors; they are the colors opposite each other on the color circle in which the hues are arranged in spectral order as spoke-like segments of a wheel. Blue and yellow, red and blue-green, and violet and yellow-green are some examples. Complementary colors are those that differ most from one another and are the most contrasting. The complement of any color can be identified easily be staring at the color for thirty seconds or so and then looking at a white wall. What is then seen is the negative afterimage—a blotch of color of the same shape as the original object but having the opposite or complementary color. If one now looks at another colored object, the negative afterimage will be superimposed upon it and change the color accordingly. Sometimes the effect is quite pervasive. If we have been sitting in a greenish room and go into a room that is painted white, the walls may take on a pinkish cast. Or, if we have been looking at a green computer screen, the images on a black-and-white television screen or the white letters on a typewriter keyboard take on a rosy hue. Neither this effect nor adaptation is likely to occur very often with foods because we do not usually stare at any one color long enough, but subtle changes can occur without our being aware of them.

Color Contrast

Adjacent colors: The apparent color of an object is affected by the color of other objects adjacent to it. In simultaneous color contrast, a color takes on a bit of the hue of the complement of the adjacent color. None of these effects is very strong, and they take place mainly along the edges where the two colors meet. If blue and blue-green are next to each other, the blue will seem to have a bit of red added to it and will appear slightly blue-violet. The blue-green will look a bit more yellow-green. If blue and yellow are put next to each other, both colors will look more highly colored because the blue takes on a bit more blue and the yellow takes on a bit more yellow. Yellow next to yellow will look more grayish and less bright because each yellow will take on some blue and when blue light is mixed with yellow light, gray is produced.

Background colors: Simultaneous color-contrast effects are stronger when a colored object or area is surrounded by a colored background. The effect is due to inhibition, and the principles of color mixture apply. Simply stated, the color of the background decreases the apparent amount of that color in the object. Yellow on a yellow background looks less yellow than on a background with no yellow in it and will look most yellow on a blue background. The less yellow in the background, the more yellow the object will seem. Red will look less red on a red background. Purple that is made up of blue and red will look bluer or less red on a red background and redder or more red-violet on a blue background. Orange will look paler (less red) on a red background and deeper on a yellow one.

Application to foods: Simultaneous color contrast suggests that foods can be arranged in combinations so that their colors are subtly enhanced, subdued, or otherwise modified. Yellow scrambled eggs on a yellow plate will look paler because of contrast. Purple grapes will look less purple on a purple plate and will look redder on a blue plate. A green salad will look less green on a green plate than on a plate that has no green in it. Red food on a blue plate will look more orange. Broccoli served with red fish will make the fish look redder, and slices of lime surrounding a grape mousse will enhance the color of both.

Color Combinations

Accent colors: Chefs aim for color interest. Bright, saturated colors are good for accent. A dash of paprika, a slice of orange, a serving of carrots, or sprigs of bright green parsley add color and interest, but they should be used with less pure, duller colors and they must be less distinctive in size and shape than what they are accenting or they lose their effectiveness. Bright colors usually are not good accents for other bright colors, and dark, deep colors are usually not effectively accented by pale, washed-out ones unless the contrast is very great and the accented item clearly dominates the garnish or decoration.

Color pairings: Some colors seem to go together quite naturally while others do not. A number of years ago interior decorators never used blue and green together; now such color schemes are commonplace. This shows that the pleasingness of color combinations is affected by learning and familiarity. Out of long tradition, some combinations are preferred to others, such as red and green for Christmas and yellow and lavender for Easter. The acceptability of yellow and lavender carries over in clothing and interior decoration, but, with few exceptions, the red and green combination does not. The colors are too strong and bright to work together.

Color Combinations in Foods

In food as in other uses of color, some color combinations are preferred to others. The color of red cabbage cole slaw does not seem to go with the red of boiled beets. Some colors fit particular foods because of learning and associations and the meanings the colors convey. Dark green parsley looks healthy; yellow-green parsley looks old and unattractive. On the other hand, dark green lettuce may look old and tough while yellow-green lettuce seems fresh and tender.

Colors should not clash nor should they be monotonous. Breast of chicken in a cream sauce served with mashed potatoes and yellow string beans, or even made fancy with Belgian endive, looks boring because there is no color contrast. The same chicken served with a baked potato and sliced carrots has interest because of contrast in color and form.

Dark and Light Colors

Dark colors, like pure bright ones, signify strength, and combinations of dark colors are occasionally acceptable in foods, provided they fit the other meanings being conveyed. A meal of steak, sliced beets, a baked potato, and a contrasting tossed salad conveys robustness, but if fried potatoes are substituted for the baked potato, the impression becomes one of heaviness.

The principle of fittingness also applies to combinations of light colors.

Delicacy and lightness are conveyed by pale colors but, unless one is trying to produce a special effect, paleness may be uninteresting. A pale omelet served with mashed potatoes and green beans has little color appeal, although the form and texture of the beans make them a better choice than creamed onions. Light colors need shape and texture contrasts in order to avoid the impression of blandness. Poached whitefish served with broccoli, peas, or beets seems more flavorful than if served with spinach or mashed carrots. Peas, broccoli, and beets have definite forms and textures that contrast with the fish. The color of the carrots is not enough to compensate for their amorphous shape and texture. Sliced or whole baby carrots would add interest to the serving.

The worst possible combinations are light colors, soft textures, and bland foods. Instead of conveying light airiness, they convey weakness and evoke boredom. They are the worst possible combinations for the sick and infirm. In care facilities, such combinations often are served on white plates and drab trays. They have all the characteristics of baby food and are perceived that way. They enhance feelings of weakness and dependence and often evoke feelings of resentment and hostility toward those giving care. Sometimes, of course, soft, bland foods or even liquids are necessary diets, but there is no reason to enhance those qualities by serving the foods on colorless dishes and trays. It should be possible to compensate for the lack of taste and boring sameness of texture by the judicious use of color combinations in the foods. The one occasion when bland, soft foods are psychologically desirable is when the person perceives him or herself to be "weaker" than the food. Then the perception of the food as nourishing overrides other meanings.

Modes of Appearance

In addition to hue, saturation, and brightness, or the clearness, paleness, dullness, and lightness of colors, colors have other visual characteristics known as *modes of appearance* (Katz 1935). Two of these are *volume color* and *surface* (or *object*) *color*. Volume color is transparent and translucent rather than opaque. Consommé and gelatin desserts are good examples. Surface color, as the name implies, is seen as being on a surface or being the color of a solid object. In food it is seen only on the surface or at cut edges. Sometimes the surface color is different from the interior, but the surface color combined with other qualities gives an impression of the interior. The burned surface of rare steak looks shinier and moister than the burned surface of well-done steak.

With some foods, such as consommés, jellies, and some sauces, volume color is highly desirable because it indicates clarity, purity, lightness, fragility, or careful preparation. Cloudiness suggests improper preparation or the presence of solids or residues that should have been removed. On the other hand, when gravies, jams, or the juice of berry pies have volume color, one also assumes lack of care in preparation. Then, however, one believes that solids and residues that should have been present either were removed or were absent in the first place. One assumes that shortcut cooking methods were used, with cornstarch or pectin added to thicken a watery base and make up for the lack of substance.

Volume colors, like blues or grays, are relatively rare in foods in their natural states. They are appealing therefore only if the foods have some special characteristics that set them apart, such as delicacy or the knowledge that skill and care were required in their preparation.

Color Preferences
Preferred Colors

The color most preferred by children six to twenty-four months of age is red, followed by yellow, blue, and green; in later preschool years, the order is red, blue, green, and yellow. In early grade school the order is blue, red, green, and yellow. Later and into adulthood blue and green are preferred more than any others (Dember and Warm 1979). Young children prefer strong, bright colors, and this holds true in their choices of candies and desserts. By adolescence, pastels are preferred (Zubek and Solberg 1954). Few teenagers or adults would want a red birthday cake. Generally, saturated or pure colors are preferred to "muddy" or grayish ones.

Fairly consistent relations exist between menu-item categories and the pleasantness of odors as well as the heaviness of textures. The relation is much less clear for colors. Warm colors usually are preferred for main dishes, with the exception of reds. Cool colors are liked more often in salads and desserts, but there are many exceptions. Perhaps the most likely order of items from darkest to lightest is main dish, vegetables, soups, desserts, and salads, but the order can vary a great deal because of the subtlety and diversity of colors.

Color versus Shape

When given different forms of various colors and instructed to match or sort them, preschool children over three years of age usually make the matches on the basis of color and ignore shape. Children under the age of three show a preference for form, and school-age children and adults match forms and tend to ignore color (Thompson 1962). The tendency is dominant by the age of six, although some individuals continue to be primarily color- rather than form-reactors (Honkavaara 1958). Perhaps this explains why some very young children and some older children and adults are so fussy about how their food is cut or served.

The dominance of form over color suggests that form has more meaning than color, and this is generally true. We group houses, books, flowers, or dishes on the basis of shape rather than color. A house is a house whether it is white, green, or yellow. With foods, however, color is often as important as shape in determining meaning. Peas are peas because of their shape, but they are peas and not tapioca because of their color. Corn is corn whether on the cob, whole-kernel, or creamed; and gray-green canned peas are simply not the same food as fresh-cooked ones. Perhaps color is more important because many foods can be served in a variety of ways. Carrots can be sliced, diced, mashed, or served whole, but they are still perceived as carrots because of their color. Form is used to identify foods that are usually served in the same way; form tells us that broccoli is different from spinach, and that cookies are different from muffins. Since so many other foods are served in different ways, color rather than form becomes the more important basis for identification.

Color Meanings
Bright and Pale Colors

Bright, saturated, warm colors usually mean strength, but not always. In a study of capsule color and medicine strength, red and black capsules were believed to contain the strongest medicine and white capsules the weakest, with yellow, green, blue, and orange somewhere in between (Sallis and Buckalew 1984). Capsule color also had other meanings. Red and yellow capsules were judged to contain stimulants, and blue ones to contain depressants (Jacobs and Nordan 1979). This fits the general view that red, yellow, and orange are active colors while blue and green are inactive or passive. In another study, detergent packaged in a yellow-orange box was rated as too strong and harsh; that in a blue box as too weak; and that in a blue and yellow-orange box as most appropriate. The ratings were made after use, and the same detergent was in all boxes (Kupchella 1976).

Pale colors suggest a lack of flavor, as in pale pink watermelon or a pale-chocolate devil's-food cake. On the other hand, clear, bright, highly saturated colors are not common in nature, and highly saturated red in cherry pie looks artificial as does bright, clear yellow chicken gravy. Bright red strawberry Jello is itself a manufactured food, so an artificial red may be appropriate; also, we are so accustomed to the color of Jello that a light red would seem bland and flavorless.

Although pale colors look weak, faded, and washed-out if they are improperly used, they have a delicate and fragile air when combined with appropriate textures and forms. A pale lemon-yellow chiffon is much more attractive than a deep yellow chiffon because the color fits the lightness of texture. For the same reason, a deep, rich, highly saturated chocolate soufflé is not as appealing as a somewhat lighter one. With devil's-food cake, or char-broiled steak, the darker the better. Dark, deep, highly saturated colors look strong and hearty, but their acceptability in food depends on the food in question. The dark yellow yolks in eggs from grass-fed chickens are less attractive than pale yellow yolks and almost seem unhealthy because we are accustomed to the latter.

Our response to foods from which color has been removed is almost universally negative if we are familiar with the original color. Cooking some fruits and vegetables and overcooking others tends to leach out color and flavor; the colors lose saturation and become grayish. Canned peas and raspberries and thawed frozen strawberries are examples. When color-desaturated foods do not look natural, we associate the loss of color with loss in flavor—a relationship confirmed by experience. Probably there is also an unlearned aspect in our negative response to foods that tend toward gray. Not only is it an unnatural color in foods, but it is a neutral color and does not attract attention or create interest or curiosity. It may also suggest contamination. Perhaps that is why bleached flour and white sugar have been in vogue and all kinds of additives from ashes to lime have been used to make white bread whiter. Because gray is unnatural and associated with lack of flavor, it cannot be used to advantage as a background or contrast color in food as it often is in clothing or interior decoration.

Color and Emotions

Among both contemporary and primitive societies, colors have always had symbolic or emotional meanings. Some meanings are universal while others vary with the culture: white or black can be for mourning or celebration. Although forms or shapes are likely to have intellectual meanings, colors are more likely to have emotional ones (Birren 1969), and our language is full of examples in which color words are used to describe emotions: green with envy, purple with rage, red with anger or embarrassment, and blue with sorrow.

There is general agreement among artists (Hevner 1935), color theorists, and applied psychologists that different mood tones tend to go with different colors (Birren 1969). Although there are individual differences, generally a majority of individuals match the same colors to the same emotions (Wexner 1954). The results of one study, showing the emotions that did and did not go with specific colors, are given in table 10-1 (Schaie 1961).

The results, like those from most such studies, are based on showing the colors on neutral backgrounds. In the everyday world, the meanings of colors, like the meanings of odors and shapes, are affected by the setting or context in which they occur. In the Anglican and Roman churches, for example, red stands for martyrdom, a meaning not too unlike the usual ones of danger, injury, or death. In health-care settings, red, blue, black, and purple may be associated with fear, pain, and death. Yellow suggests the sallow complexion of jaundice or disease (Pierman 1978). In other settings, it may imply neurosis or cowardice, and at still other times it may mean joy and gaiety.

Food as a Complex Psychological Stimulus

TABLE 10-1. Descriptive scheme for the association between colors and
mood-tones

Color	Strong association	Little or no association
Red	protective, defending; power-ful, strong, masterful; (excit-ing, stimulating)*	Calm, peaceful, serene; tender, soothing
Orange	exciting, stimulating	calm, peaceful, serene; tender, soothing; dignified, stately
Yellow	exciting, stimulating; cheerful, jovial, joyful; pleasant	dignified, stately; despondent, dejected, melancholy, un-happy; protective, defending; powerful, strong, masterful
Green		dignified, stately; protective, defending; powerful, strong, masterful; despondent, de-jected, melancholy, unhappy
Blue	pleasant; secure, comfortable; tender, soothing; (calm, peaceful, serene; exciting, stimulating)	distressed, disturbed, upset; despondent, dejected, melan-choly, unhappy; defiant, contrary, hostile
Purple	dignified, stately; (despondent, dejected, melancholy, un-happy)	exciting, stimulating; cheerful, jovial, joyful
Brown	(secure, comfortable)	cheerful, jovial, joyful; defiant, contrary, hostile; exciting, stimulating; powerful, strong, masterful; pleasant
White	tender, soothing; (calm, peace-ful, serene)	exciting, stimulating; despon-dent, dejected, melancholy, unhappy; defiant, contrary, hostile; distressed, disturbed, upset; powerful, strong, masterful
Gray	despondent, dejected, melan-choly, unhappy (calm, peace-ful, serene)	exciting, stimulating; defiant, contrary, hostile; powerful, strong, masterful; cheerful, jovial, joyful
Black	distressed, disturbed, upset; defiant, contrary, hostile; despondent, dejected, melan-choly, unhappy; dignified, stately; powerful, strong, masterful	exciting, stimulating; secure, comfortable; tender, sooth-ing; cheerful, jovial, joyful; calm, peaceful, serene; pleas-ant

* Parentheses indicate moderate associations or mood-tones whose scalar order varied between the two groups of judges.

Reprinted by permission from: Schaie, K. W. (1961). Scaling the association between colors and mood-tones. *American Journal of Psychology*, 74: 266–73. © University of Illinois Press.

Color and Flavor

We tend to associate certain colors with particular flavors, usually, but not always, because the colors match the colors of the foods from which they come. A list of these associations is shown in table 10-2 (Nieman 1961; Walford 1980).

The relation between color and flavor can be strong enough to reverse flavor impressions. In a taste study, trained testers identified chocolate-flavored white ice cream as vanilla and chocolate-colored vanilla ice cream as chocolate; in another study, children believed red gelatins were strawberry and yellow ones were lemon, regardless of the actual flavor (Walford 1980). It is likely that mistaking or confusing flavors would occur much more often if colors were not present to give flavor cues. Color also has other effects on taste or flavor. It was noted in the chapter on taste (chapter 6) that a more deeply colored orange juice was judged sweeter than a pale one, although careful tests suggested that the difference in taste was more imagined than real (Schutz 1954). Further, the judged pleasantness of orange juice decreases if the color becomes too deep (Pangborn 1984). Oranges with partly green skins do not seem to taste as sweet as bright orange ones even though the latter may be colored artificially. Sometimes, however, positive eye appeal evokes an expectation which if not fulfilled results in a negative reaction to the food. If it is not crisp and sweet, a large, brightly colored Red Delicious apple is a greater disappointment than a smaller, less colored one. The visually less appealing apple may "taste" better because less flavor was expected. The same effect is found in odors. Hot chocolate that smells rich and sweet will be a disappointment if it is thin and watery.

TABLE 10-2. **Association between popular flavors and colors**

Apricot	Pale golden yellow	Mint	Yellow-green
Blackberry Blackcurrant	Dark bluish red	Orange	Bright reddish orange
Butterscotch	Golden brown	Peach	Light dull gold
Cassia	Dark red	Peppermint	White
Cherry	Bright bluish red	Pineapple	Greenish yellow
Chocolate	Dark reddish brown	Pistachio	Bright green
Clove	Light red	Plum	Reddish navy
Honey	Golden yellow	Prune	Dark navy
Lemon	Greenish or canary yellow	Raspberry	Bright bluish red
Liquorice	Dark blackish brown	Spearmint	Medium green
Lime	Bright bluish green	Strawberry	Bright bluish pink

Reprinted by permission from: Walford, J. (1980). Historical development of food coloration. In J. Walford, ed., *Developments in food colours—1*. London: Applied Science Publishers. (Originally compiled from Nieman, C. (1961). *Colours recently authorised in 43 countries*. Amsterdam.)

As with hue, the impression conveyed by the color saturation level of foods depends on the combination of colors, textures, flavors, and shapes. It also depends on the extent to which the saturation is natural and the extent to which it has become customary for particular foods.

To many people, brown-shelled eggs "taste" better than white-shelled eggs even though their flavors are identical and the eggs could not be told apart without knowing their shell color. The preference may have more to do with color associations than with the actual color, although white (and black) is a least-liked color (Guilford 1934). Brown eggs are laid by breeds of chickens such as Rhode Island Reds or Buff Orpingtons that are not such prolific layers as those that lay white eggs. Consequently, brown eggs are rarely produced on a large scale, coming mostly from small farms. Further, brown-egg layers are usually heavier; when many families had their own chickens, these breeds were favored because they made plumper fryers and roasters. Whether the preference for brown eggs is due to their scarcity, their warmer earth color which makes them seem more nutritious, or the association with farm and country is not clear. The reasons may vary from person to person, but it seems likely that the color is important not only because it may evoke all those associations but also because white is often associated with lack of flavor. Except for milk, most white foods do not signify health, although high-quality protein ingredients also are usually light in color and have a bland flavor (Cherry 1981).

Food-Color Preferences

General color preferences are not directly applicable to color preferences in foods. Blue is unnatural in foods, and although it is a preferred color, it is not enjoyed in foods, except perhaps for Popsicles and bubble gum, and these are rarely bought by adults. It is used only sparingly even in decorating cakes. Nor is green a favorite food color. The thought of green meat is abhorrent. Although tossed salads are primarily green, and so are some vegetables, neither of these tops the list of preferred foods; usually, but not always, they are ranked lower than other menu items (Lyman 1982a).

If preferences for independent colors do not carry over to color preferences in foods, what role do colors play in food preferences? Do they affect choices, and are they related to palatability? The answer is clearly yes, although learning and experience and the meanings that colors have for food quality seem more important than color preferences alone. Familiarity and associations play a role, as they do in food preferences generally, and a large part of familiarity has to do with the colors being natural for specific foods and naturally associated with specific qualities.

The relation between food preferences and earth and sky colors is an example. Earth colors—greens, browns, and dark yellows—are preferred in fruits and vegetables and meats that feed off the land, especially when these are served rather plainly without embellishment. They are somewhat less desirable in complexly prepared or manufactured foods such as desserts or bakery goods. But even here brown crusts are desired, and browning agents are used in preparing many foods in microwave cooking. Earth colors are natural to many foods, and perhaps this natural relation accounts for the food-color preference; or there may be some deep-seated association between color and nurture and the bounties of the earth.

Sky colors, such as blue, white, gray, and pastel pinks and yellow-reds, are not common in natural foods and are not well regarded in main-dish items in Western culture. They are used mainly in light foods and in desserts, or as decorative additions to other foods as garnishes, frostings, chaud-froids, and sauces. However, there is a major exception. Sky colors and pastels are acceptable in main courses of seafoods—white halibut, pink shrimp, or crab, for example. These are the foods' natural colors; but, also, sea creatures do not feed on the land, and sky colors are often reflected in the ocean or associated with ocean sunsets. Perhaps the greater use of pastels in Japanese cooking is related to that nation's closeness to the sea, although English food is not noted for pastels, and England too is a sea-bound nation. Traditionally, however, there is less seafood in the English diet, and perhaps the harsher northern climate requires warmer, heavier colors.

Throughout the discussions of the sensory qualities of food the importance of food meanings is implied or clearly stated. The major source of those meanings is the associations that foods have with objects, people, places, and situations. This is the subject of the following chapter.

PART 4

Food Meanings and Associations

CHAPTER 11

Food Meanings

The appearance, flavor, and texture of food are directly experienced as sensory qualities in their own right, and the perception of these qualities is modified by the physical and mental contexts in which they occur. Food's real impact on the fullness of mental life, however, comes from the variety and complexity of its associations and the images, thoughts, ideas, and feelings it evokes. It is these sensory and nonsensory contexts and associations that give food its meaning. Through associations, a specific food or some sensory component of it reminds us of something other than the food itself, and because our responses to food are governed as much or more by its meaning as by its sensory qualities, the associations have effects that go far beyond purely nutritional ones. The physical characteristics of objects are important, but the responses of both adults and children are dominated by the meanings of the objects (Osgood 1952; Siegel 1954).

Meaning and Imagery
The Core-Context Theory of Meaning

According to the core-context theory, meaning is given to a stimulus by the context of images in which the sensory experience occurs. Sensations are the direct result of receptor stimulation in the present, but images are not. Historically, images were defined as faint copies of sensations, but that definition should not be taken too literally. Current definitions are more general, and an image is often defined as a centrally aroused sensation or a perception-like experience in the absence of a real object (Ahsen 1986). The word itself is derived from the Latin *imitare*—to imitate–and has to do with the literal meaning of the word *imagination*, which the American Heritage Dictionary defines as "the act or power of forming a mental image of something not present to the senses." We can experience the flavor of a pear as sensation or we can experience it in memory or imagination as an image. The sensory qualities of the object are the basis for identification and recognition, but the context of mental contents in which that sensation occurs gives it its particular meaning, which may be peculiar to us or shared by others.

Psychological, as opposed to optical or photographic, images are usually copies, reconstructions, or recollections of sensory experience and have the same attributes as sensations: differences in kind, clarity, intensity, duration, and extensity. Although images are defined as "faint copies," sometimes they have a strength and intensity that rivals the sensations themselves, as when one is willing to swear that the doorbell has rung when it has not or that there are cookies baking in the oven when there is nothing at all being baked.

Images

Kinds of images: Images often are classified as either memory or fantasy images (Arnold 1984). The most common are *memory images,* which, as the name implies, are recollections of some past experience. They can be as simple as the memory of a sound or a bit of color or they can be as complex as memories of dinner with a friend or travels through Europe. *Fantasy images* are "created" and are not simple recollections of past experience. They may be reconstructions or new combinations of bits and pieces from various memories, or they may represent something never before experienced.

Memory changes in images: Because images may occur hours or even years after the sensations from which they derive, they are subject to distortion when being recalled into consciousness (Bartlett 1932). With the passage of time, sharpening may take place so that in memory some of the characteristics of the object or situation become clearer and more intense than the original experience. The cherries we stole as children really were not that sweet, and the parsnips we refused to eat did not really make us gag. Leveling also may occur, so that less important aspects drop from memory, to be recalled only with concentration and difficulty. Other changes also take place. The most common are distortions to simplify the meaning or to make the memory more sensible by forgetting contradictions.

Images and expectations: Images can wreak havoc with diets and eating behavior. Food may be rejected or refused not because of its actual taste or smell but because some negative qualities of it have been exaggerated in memory. Sometimes, if we can be induced to try something we thought we did not like, we are surprised to find it is quite pleasant and not at all what we remembered it to be. On the other hand, positive sharpening may lead to disappointment with the actual food. In memory, the tastiness of a particular item may be so exaggerated that it is beyond the realm of possibility for an actual dish ever to match our expectations. Was mother's cooking really all that great?

By creating contradictions between expectation and reality, well-meaning parents often defeat their own efforts to get their children to eat nutritionally desirable foods. Telling them that the lukewarm mashed squash is delicious builds an expectation and imaginary taste that is completely demolished by the first bite, and the contrast between expectation and reality actually makes the squash seem even less tasty than it actually is.

Images, Thoughts, and Ideas

Meaning and memory have been discussed above in terms of images, but apparently not all individuals have mental images, or at least some say they do not. Some psychologists argue that thoughts and ideas are a separate category of conscious material. Others argue that if we concentrated or reflected long enough on thoughts and even abstract ideas we would find that they ultimately reduce to images or sensory experience of some kind. For many people, visual images accompany the idea of going to the store or the thought of eating dinner. Similarly, it is difficult for many people to think of such abstract concepts as fairness, brotherhood, or trust without at the same time picturing concrete situations to which the concepts and beliefs apply. Other individuals are less image-prone. Some tend to think in abstract ideas, and there are reports of individuals who rarely, if ever, have any imagery at all.

Associations

Although the argument regarding the nature of thought is interesting for the student of psychology, it need not concern us here. The essential point is that food is a sensory stimulus which like all stimuli evokes for most people a host of images, thoughts, ideas, and feelings. It is these that give food its meaning, and the effect occurs whether one has images or imageless thoughts. Substituting the word *associations* for "images" and "thoughts" and the other components of the experienced context emphasizes this fact as well as the idea that a variety of mental states or activities is involved. Associations run through every shade and nuance of human experience. Some are simple and obvious while others are so subtle and complex that we become aware of them only under very exceptional circumstances or discover them only by careful and prolonged reflection.

Unlearned Associations

Some associations are direct and unlearned. One food reminds us of another because of some actual similarity in the two. The sweet-sourness of fresh pineapple may remind us of an orange. Ripe quinces may remind us of Golden Delicious apples until we try to eat one. The slipperiness of raw oysters may make us think of raw eggs. Not all unlearned sensory associations are between one food and another. The seed pods of the golden chain tree look like green string beans, and many children have been poisoned by eating them. Some children delight in pearl tapioca because it is fish eyes to them; some adults abhor it for the same reason.

Unlearned associations are much more widespread than is commonly recognized. They are part of the basis for universal or shared associations in which a given object evokes, without learning, the same thoughts or ideas in persons from very different cultures or backgrounds.

Like all associations, when they are strong and clear, they make us immediately aware of why we like or dislike some particular food, but when they are weak, the reasons for our likes and dislikes elude us and we are left with some vague awareness that there is "something about the taste" or "something about the odor" that we find pleasant or do not like.

Learned Associations

Most associations are acquired or learned. One food reminds us of another because the two have been paired together in the past. Usually this is because they have been served together or eaten at the same meal, but there are many other possibilities. They may have been seen together on the same shelf, or both may be recognized as being expensive. Learned associations may be peculiar to only one person or they may be shared by a large number of people because of similar experiences. To many Americans, the smell of frying bacon triggers off the thought of coffee, eggs, and toast. To those who like liver, the smell of it cooking may evoke thoughts of bacon or fried onions.

Like unlearned associations, learned associations may be clear or vague or strong or weak. For food, their strength depends primarily on the frequency and the consistency with which the foods or other associations occurred together in the past. If liver was served only once with onions, the thought or presence of one would be unlikely to trigger off the idea of the other. If there was only one minor disagreement over breakfast cereal, it is unlikely that cooked cereal would be disliked for that reason. There are exceptions to this, of course. Sometimes an experience is so dramatic or so novel that a strong association develops from a single pairing. If one's first experience with beaten biscuits is at a country ham dinner, it is likely the two will be associated for a long time. Or, if a North American were served kippers and scrambled eggs at a wedding breakfast, the novelty would almost certainly ensure a lifetime connection between the two.

Learned associations, like unlearned ones, need not be between one food and another. Many of today's older adults will not eat cooked breakfast cereal because of the memory of breakfast battles when it was forced on them as children. Most of us associate sauerkraut with frankfurters or a Reuben sandwich, but, as noted earlier, to those who grew up on Maryland's Eastern Shore, sauerkraut means roast goose and Christmas dinner because it is a traditional part of that meal.

Some associations are hidden deep in the unconscious and go back to earliest childhood and half-forgotten nursery rhymes and other stories. Many of these have references to food: Jack Spratt, Little Jack Horner, Little Miss Muffet, Simple Simon, the poisoned apple in Snow White, Cinderella's pumpkin, and Jack's beanstalk are but a few. Since some of the rhymes and stories are read to children while they are still in their cradles, the associations may exist unrecognized but still affect attitudes toward specific foods.

Complex Associations

The associations that have the most far-reaching and profound psychological effects are those in which food awakens complex memories and activates a whole set of ideas, thoughts, images, and feelings. These may be relatively simple, involving a single memory, or whole scenes may flood into consciousness—Proust's recollections aroused by Madeleines are the classic example. Lobster bisque may mean only a girl named Frances or it may include the whole elegant atmosphere of Montreal's Ritz Carleton Hotel because of a dinner once eaten there with her. The recollection of breakfast battles over cooked cereal may be simple and direct, or there may be a flood of childhood memories going far beyond the breakfast table.

The images occurring in complex associations may not be recollections of actual experiences. Cabbage soup may create a picture of French peasants around a table eating supper in a warm and humble cottage even though we have never been to France or seen a French peasant. The images may come about because we first heard of cabbage soup when studying French, or they may represent some complex combination of images, thoughts, and ideas gleaned from a variety of unrecognized sources. (*Glean* is not the best word here, because we do not actively seek the images and thoughts; they simply come upon us. Perhaps the word came to mind because of the association between cabbage soup and French peasants and between French peasants and the gleaners in Millet's painting of that name.)

Association Sequences

The relation between food and complex associations is complicated further by the fact that chains of associations can occur in which food, actually present or imagined, or some sensory component of it, evokes imagery and ideas and these evoke other images and ideas which evoke still other images and ideas to form a sequence of associations far removed from the original stimulus. The chain of associations arising from lobster bisque at the Ritz Carleton fans out in a dozen different directions—the shops on Sherbrooke Street, an expensive watch in one of these, a rooming house on old Pierce Street, a drugstore counter at Peel and St. Catherine, listening to the Kentucky Derby in the Royal Victoria Hospital, then the Blue Grass Room in Lexington, Kentucky, the Keeneland sales, Tates Creek Pike in

October, a soprano singing German lieder, Henry Clay and his "I know only my country," the American Congress, Washington, D.C., in a sweltering August, and on and on—all this from a little cup of soup!

Associations have been discussed as if they occurred only when food was present, but neither sight, nor smell, nor taste is necessary. Sensations, by definition, are never present without the food stimulus, but images, thoughts, ideas, feelings, and other associations can occur when simply thinking of the food or hearing its name; or they can occur spontaneously. The relations between sensations, foods, and associations, whether unlearned or learned, may be summarized briefly as follows.

1) Either an actual *sensation* (such as an odor, taste, or color) or an imagined one reminds us of some other sensation or creates an image or thought of some food. Feelings may also be evoked. The real or imagined sensation may or may not be a sensory quality of some specific food. The astringent or puckery quality of alum may remind us of unripe persimmons or the bitter taste of medicine. The odor of dill can make us think of pickles or the sourness of vinegar.

2) The *sensation stimulus* in (1) may evoke some simple or complex association other than a food. The association may include a feeling or emotion. Thus, the odor of dill could result in our imagining the plant, or we could think of an herb garden. In *Julia Child and Company*, Ms. Child writes, "I can't taste Indian pudding without thinking of it simmering all of an iron-hard January afternoon, slowly releasing its comfortable spicy scent into a cold dark little cabin. It must have hit the spot for frozen weary people who'd been hacking all day at the endless forest" (Child 1978).

3) A *specific food* item (rather than its real or imagined sensory qualities), or the thought or image of it, may remind us of a sensation or of some other food, or it may evoke simple or complex nonfood associations. Again, feelings and emotions may be involved. These are the broadest kinds of associations and the ones through which food has its greatest psychological effects.

Associations and Food Preferences

The importance of associations in food preferences and selections is widely recognized (Bass et al. 1979; Fleck 1981; Gifft et al. 1976; King 1980) and is used by the restaurant trade: "Peasant food reminds patrons of European travels, fills a need for new dining treats, and allows operators to romanticize low-cost foods" (Institutions 1979). In spite of this recognition, there are no studies identifying concretely the specific associations evoked by various foods. Some food meanings such as masculine, feminine or baby, adult or old have been reported (Bass et al. 1979), and dimensions of healthfulness, nutritiveness, personal use, and psychosocial or emotional meanings have been reported for a few foods (Prattala and Keinonen 1984).

Current Research

A study was carried out by the author to collect information regarding the specific associations going with different foods. The full study has not yet been published.

As a take-home project, 29 university students were given one of three lists of 48 different foods such as roast beef, baked squash, and butter-scotch pudding. A total of 87 students and 144 different food items was involved. The students were asked to take the time to imagine as clearly as possible each food as a ready-to-eat serving and then to record everything that came to mind. The use of imagination simulates real-world conditions where we often think about food before actually seeing it. They were also asked to indicate whether they liked, disliked, or felt neutral about each item.

Results: For each food, the association or image referents shown in table 11-1 were identified and the results tallied in terms of the percent of liked, disliked, and neutral food responses having each kind of association. These results are shown for menu-item categories in tables 11-1, 11-2, and 11-3.

Clearly, there are differences in the percents of various referents depending on the food category and whether the food was liked, disliked, or neutral. Statistical analyses done on the *frequencies* of referents showed significantly more associations for liked than for disliked or neutral foods. The average number of referents per item was 2.4 for liked foods and 1.8 for disliked and neutral foods. These figures are probably much too small. Ideally, taped personal interviews would have been used to ensure complete responses. The written responses were often much briefer than they would have been otherwise. The analyses also showed significant differences among the categories (except for fruit) in the percents of liked, disliked, and neutral food responses for which there were no associations. The percent of "no associations" was greatest for neutral foods. Neutral foods also had the largest percent of not-tried foods. This would be expected. However, the percent of not-tried foods *with* associations was largest for disliked foods (58 percent versus 17 percent for liked and 14 percent for disliked foods). This strongly suggests that foods are often disliked— although they have never been tried—because of the associations they carry.

Table 11-4 shows the extent to which referent frequencies for liked, disliked, and neutral foods contributed to the total percents in each association category. Reading across the rows shows that the percents of associations occurring with liked foods compared with disliked and neutral foods were appreciably higher for places, events, activities, weather/time, other

Food

TABLE 11-1. Percent of liked food responses having the associations listed

Association	Soup	Salad	Eggs	Sea-food	Meat	Vege-tables	Casse-roles	Fast Foods	Fruit	Dessert	Overall
Feelings	24	20	21	21	18	14	16	25	20	20	18
People	15	17	7	14	25	14	18	21	18	24	17
Places	23	32	12	39	21	21	21	59	29	23	25
Things	19	19	13	23	13	16	22	15	21	22	18
Events	10	14	17	11	25	7	12	11	5	15	12
Activities	13	25	19	30	15	10	19	21	29	19	18
Weather-Time	15	19	35	11	22	9	16	17	20	14	15
Past	6	2	6	7	4	5	6	8	5	8	5
Future	—	—	—	—	—	—	—	—	—	—	—
Other Foods	20	22	39	23	36	41	29	25	18	19	27
Characteristics	21	10	17	19	8	24	18	17	32	26	19
Preparation Method	15	5	24	20	20	22	13	20	11	7	15
Other	5	6	5	10	6	8	5	5	12	6	7
No Association	8	2	1	7	3	5	5	—	4	7	4

TABLE 11-2. Percent of disliked food responses having the associations listed

	Food										
Association	Soup	Salad	Eggs	Sea-food	Meat	Vege-tables	Casse-roles	Fast Foods	Fruit	Dessert	Overall
Feelings	29	43	38	32	30	33	34	26	55	29	33
People	10	30	13	12	11	22	19	5	5	19	17
Places	17	30	13	37	28	9	16	42	27	17	22
Things	10	17	13	17	24	20	27	11	23	16	19
Events	5	17	13	7	7	4	8	5	—	7	7
Activities	5	20	13	19	9	17	8	16	9	14	13
Weather-Time	—	—	13	8	5	7	3	5	5	8	6
Past	—	7	—	4	4	7	3	11	5	6	5
Future	—	—	—	—	—	2	—	—	—	—	—
Other Foods	7	27	38	14	22	16	14	—	5	13	15
Characteristics	31	33	50	23	25	25	27	21	14	28	26
Preparation Method	17	7	38	6	10	11	14	—	—	3	9
Other	3	7	13	4	14	9	11	11	27	6	9
No Association	19	3	—	6	1	11	6	5	9	8	8

TABLE 11-3. Percent of neutral food responses having the associations listed

Association	Soup	Salad	Eggs	Sea-food	Meat	Vege-tables	Casse-roles	Fast Foods	Fruit	Dessert	Overall
								Food			
Food Association	2	2	—	2	2	3	3	—	8	4	—
Feelings	26	24	22	16	18	13	24	38	27	18	20
People	8	21	13	11	17	15	20	12	29	15	16
Places	15	19	13	19	18	16	7	35	15	18	17
Things	7	19	13	20	13	11	16	27	20	17	16
Events	3	10	13	6	7	7	4	12	2	9	7
Activities	10	12	13	14	9	5	12	21	21	9	11
Weather-Time	5	12	26	4	6	9	10	9	18	8	8
Past	—	7	22	8	5	3	4	6	6	3	5
Future	2	—	4	—	2	—	—	—	—	1	—
Other Foods	5	24	17	9	22	29	7	9	9	11	14
Characteristics	21	19	22	21	13	29	17	24	27	21	21
Preparation Method	5	5	4	17	18	16	5	9	6	6	11
Other	7	10	22	6	8	6	10	12	11	4	7
No Association	26	12	9	24	15	20	26	—	6	20	19

TABLE 11-4. Percent of frequencies in each preference category
contributing to the total frequencies in each referent category

	Valence			
Association	Liked	Disliked	Neutral	Total
Feelings	30	43	26	99
People	38	26	36	100
Places	44	29	27	100
Things	39	28	32	99
Events	48	25	27	100
Activities	43	28	29	100
Weather/Time	52	18	30	100
Past	38	28	34	100
Future	6	40	54	100
Other Foods	52	24	24	100
Physical Characteristics	29	37	34	100
Preparation Method	47	20	33	100
Other	32	32	36	100

foods, and method of preparation; they were appreciably lower for future time and physical characteristics. For disliked foods compared with liked and neutral foods, the percent for feelings was high and the percents for people and weather/time were low.

When the frequencies of the different associations were converted to percentages of the total number of associations within a preference category, there were above-chance differences in the kinds of referents across preference categories for feelings, people, events, weather/time, other foods, physical characteristics, and method of preparation (table 11-5).

Discussion: The pattern of associations that emerges for liked foods suggests a varied breadth of associations with emphases on other foods and social situations. For disliked foods, the associations are focused on feelings and the physical characteristics of the foods. The pattern of associations for neutral foods is somewhat more like that for disliked than for liked foods. For all three categories, fewer than 35 percent of the associations had anything at all to do with food (other foods, physical characteristics, or method of preparation). Examination of individual differences showed that individuals who had many food likes and few dislikes had fewer physical-characteristics associations than did those with more food dislikes. In other words, those with many food dislikes are more likely to pay attention to the physical characteristics of both liked and disliked foods, whereas for other individuals physical characteristics come to mind mainly for disliked foods.

A plausible explanation for the greater number of overall associations and fewer physical-characteristics referents with liked than with disliked or

TABLE **11-5. Percent of frequencies in each referent category contributing to the total frequencies in each preference category**

	Valence		
Association	Liked	Disliked	Neutral
Feelings	9	21	12
People	9	7	10
Places	13	10	10
Things	9	9	9
Events	6	3	4
Activities	8	7	7
Weather/Time	7	3	6
Past	2	2	2
Future	—	—	1
Other Foods	15	9	9
Physical Characteristics	10	20	19
Preparation Method	7	4	6
Other	4	5	5
Total	99	100	100

neutral foods is that since the latter are probably eaten less often, fewer associations will develop, and if the reasons for not eating them have to do with their physical characteristics or with unpleasant emotional experiences, there will be relatively more of those associations than of other kinds of associations. It is also possible that the patterns of associations found in liking and disliking are related in some way to pleasant and unpleasant emotions. The images occurring with pleasant emotions are significantly less bound to the stimulus that evokes them than is the imagery occurring with unpleasant emotions (Lyman 1984). That is consistent with the finding that references to the physical characteristics of food items were significantly less frequent with liked than with disliked foods.

Conclusions: What bearing do these findings have on food preferences? Do they help clarify the conditions responsible for them? The answer is a strong yes if one accepts the idea that what comes to mind when thinking of foods has more to do with likes and dislikes than with answers to direct questions. It seems reasonable that preferences should be linked to the characteristics of foods, and, indeed, the characteristics of foods are the reasons given when individuals are asked why they like one food and dislike another, but those may be conventional reasons rather than the real ones. Saying we dislike a food because of its taste or some other physical characteristic sounds plausible and is much more acceptable than "because it reminds me of a fight with my brother." A child who is refusing to eat a particular food is less likely to be pressured if he or she says, "It doesn't taste good." And only the most conscientious parent would fail to overlook a cookie binge when a child says, "They were just so good."

Conventional answers also are often given when an individual simply does not know the reasons for the behavior. This is particularly true for children whose parents insist that they explain why they did or did not do something: "I want to know why you did that, and I want to know now." The child is forced to come up with an answer, and, not knowing the real reasons, gives an answer that is known to be acceptable—and acceptable often means conventional.

Reasons for liking or disliking particular foods often seem vague and unclear. Many of the associations go back to earliest childhood and are half-forgotten memories that come to mind only when we think about the food and free-associate, letting our minds wander to touch on the images, thoughts, and ideas with which the food is connected.

Because people often give stereotypical or evasive answers to direct questions, psychologists sometimes use indirect or "unobtrusive" measures. Ink blots are used to uncover unconscious motives or motives a person wishes to conceal, and elaborate tests, often with built-in "lie" scores to detect evasion, are used to find out whether a person is hypochondriacal or paranoid. For the same reasons, it is justifiable to believe that what a person says when asked to report what comes to mind when thinking of liked or disliked foods has more to do with the real reasons for the likes and dislikes than do answers to direct questions. If the conclusion is valid, neither liking nor disliking has much to do with the physical characteristics of foods, although disliking is significantly more affected by them than is liking.

The differences in the number of foods with associations in each category is also relevant. Their importance in food preferences is supported by the greater number of "no associations" for neutral than for either liked or disliked foods. Spontaneous comments such as "It doesn't do anything for me" or "Nothing comes to mind" occurred with neutral foods. This also suggests that the neutral quality is related to the absence of associations.

It also seems likely that not only the number but also the pleasantness or unpleasantness of the associations plays an important role in food likes and dislikes. This was not investigated, but common sense as well as student comments support the inference. Foods that might otherwise taste good are disliked because of some unpleasant association that may be remembered or forgotten. Probably bad food would not be acceptable regardless of pleasant associations, but the research described above, as well as practical experience, suggests that food preferences depend on associations that go beyond the food itself; it suggests also that food, service, and surroundings that initiate or enhance pleasant associations can be used to increase food acceptability. This may be important not only in everyday practice but also in commercial foodservice and in institutional feeding where choices and options are limited or restricted because of dietary or other considerations.

If associations with food are so pervasive, why are we not constantly bombarded by thoughts of food? (Sometimes teenagers seem to be.) After all, if beach-plum jam is associated with a summer at the beach, the beach should remind us of the jam as readily as the jam reminds us of the beach. Or, if we eat macaroni-and-cheese dinners when we are broke, either one should remind us of the other. Yet foods are more likely to remind us of complex experiences than are complex experiences to remind us of foods. The reason is simple. Summer at the beach has many associations of which beach-plum jam is only one, but the jam is associated only or primarily with summer at the beach, so that is the direction the association will take. Similarly, many thoughts occur with being broke—checkbooks, mortgage payments, heating bills, *and* macaroni and cheese. If macaroni and cheese were eaten *only* when there was no money for anything else, it would remind us of being broke, because that association is the stronger and more restricted one.

Liking or disliking specific foods seems to depend partly, then, on the kinds of associations evoked by the foods. If this is correct, it should be possible to use associations to change food preferences. This is one of the approaches discussed in the following chapter.

It was suggested in chapter 4 that the relation between foods and feelings might be used to modify feelings through appropriate selections of foods. The same possibility exists with the relation between foods and associations. If foods evoke complex patterns of images, thoughts, ideas, and attitudes, then appropriate control of food intake might modify these as well. This proposal is discussed in chapter 13.

CHAPTER 12

Changing Food Likes and Dislikes

How can food preferences be changed so that people will like foods they dislike and dislike or at least have a lessened desire for foods they already like? The answers have implications for child-rearing practices, dieting, and nutritional training and change not only among the young but among all ages and among both the healthy and the infirm.

The practical problem of changing food preferences may be to get a person to eat more vegetables, to eat less fat or sugar, or to accept a diet of salt-free foods. With the young child this may be a matter of establishing initial preferences. With the older child or adult it may involve getting rid of old preferences as well as establishing new ones. To eat more vegetables, it is not necessary to learn to like other foods less; but to accept and enjoy a salt-free diet, one must overcome a desire for foods containing salt and come to want those containing none.

Liking and Disliking
Classes of Disliked Foods

Generally, foods that are liked are ones that have been eaten and found pleasant, but foods may be disliked whether or not they have been tasted. In comparison with liked foods, there are at least five classes of disliked foods. (1) We dislike or think we dislike some foods even though they have never been tried. Sautéed brains or kidney stew are possible examples. Since the foods have never been eaten, disliking is determined by associations and ideas about the food rather than by actual taste experience. Perhaps most dislikes are in this category. (2) Some foods are disliked after they have been tried. This may be because of the taste or some other physical characteristic which very likely would not have resulted in disliking if the food had been prepared differently. Boiled turnips are not a prized vegetable, but if diced and seasoned with spices (or even onion-soup mix), they become a tasty side dish. Buttered parsnips are shunned by many, but if fried or made into chowder, they take on interest. So do eggs disguised as custard. (3) A few foods are disliked because they have become boring and overly familiar due to their having been eaten so often. Usually, the repetition is one in which the individual had little control because of financial or dietary restraints or because someone else controlled menu planning. (4) There are also a few foods that are disliked because they cause allergic or other negative physiological reactions. Unfortunately, those foods are as often liked as disliked. (5) Finally, there are those foods which may have been liked at one time but which are now disliked because eating them was accompanied by ill effects. Either the individual became ill after eating the food—although the food might not have been the cause of the illness—or the food is associated with some traumatic emotional experience. This accounts for very few food dislikes.

Regardless of the reason for wanting to change food preferences, the major task is to turn dislikes into likes, not only because there are many more classes of disliked than liked foods, but also because getting people to refrain from eating a specific food often involves getting them to substitute a disliked food for a liked one.

The Basis for Preferences

In order to bring about preference changes, it is necessary to know why we have the preferences we have in the first place—not in terms of their acquisition, but in terms of the essential basis or reasons for the preferences. As already discussed in chapter 11, in spite of the many variables associated with the development of food preferences, most people cite flavor—taste, smell, and texture—as the main reason for liking or disliking specific foods. How valid is this assumption? Are flavor and other sensory qualities really the basis for liking and disliking? If so, then changing preferences requires changing tastes or, at least, changing the pleasantness or unpleasantness associated with taste, smell, texture, and appearance.

Food's sensory qualities are relatively unimportant: The material presented in chapter 11 showed the importance of associations other than physical characteristics in food preferences. There are other reasons for doubting that liking and disliking depend on food's flavor. (1) Children, especially, are notorious for disliking foods before they have tasted them; some adults respond the same way. If likes and dislikes depended on taste, texture, or smell, they would rarely occur before the foods were tasted. (2) Often sensory qualities that are liked in the absolute are not liked as attributes in foods. Many odors that are rated pleasant in themselves are disliked in foods, and many that are rated unpleasant are liked. The sensory experiences are not changed by the fact that they derive from foods, but somehow their meanings are different. Blue is a highly preferred color, but it is extremely unpleasant in foods. In many foods, green, which is also highly preferred, is abhorrent. Again, if liking and disliking depended on sensory qualities, those foods having highly preferred qualities should be the ones most liked. Sweet tastes in the narrow sense are liked, but sweet foods may be disliked. Mild, salty tastes also are usually rated pleasant, but, except for snack foods, foods that actually taste salty usually are disliked.

Food meanings and associations: If sensory qualities in themselves are not the major determiners of likes and dislikes, what qualities are important, and what needs to be changed in order to change food preferences or—more specifically—to change dislikes into likes? Sometimes it may be as simple as getting a person to try a food that he or she has never tasted, although this is often difficult to accomplish. In other cases, the task is more complex. All those things that contribute to the development of food preferences can also contribute to their change. In chapter 2, social and cultural influences were emphasized. In chapter 3, the physical situation and the individual's physiological state were seen as important. A relation between emotions and food preferences was shown in chapter 4. In chapters 6 through 10, food's physical characteristics were discussed. Chapter 11 specifically showed the importance of food associations and meanings in food likes and dislikes, but they were either implied or specifically mentioned in all chapters.

Attitudes

More than anything else, food meanings and associations represent attitudes toward the food itself, toward its sensory qualities, or toward the physical and social context in which it is served, including other individuals who serve or eat it.

Changing food preferences becomes a matter of changing attitudes toward foods rather than changing the pleasantness or unpleasantness of their sensory qualities or tastes.

Definitions

Attitudes, like many concepts in psychology, are defined differently by different psychologists (Worchel and Cooper 1983). Most often, the differences have to do with the scope of the concept. For some psychologists, an attitude consists only of a positive or negative feeling for or against something like an object, person, group, or idea (Thurstone 1946). An evaluation is made, usually in terms of good or bad, liked or disliked, or desirable or undesirable.

Other psychologists suggest that an attitude consists of a value or feeling component and a belief or cognitive component. A conclusion derived from the combination of the two is an attitude (Worchel and Cooper 1983). For example: vegetables do not taste good; peas are a vegetable; therefore, peas do not taste good. Foods high in nutritional value are desirable; green vegetables are nutritious; therefore, green vegetables are desirable. Or, the foods my parents have said are good for me are ones I do not like; they say this food is good for me; therefore, I will not like it. The conclusions express attitudes toward peas, green vegetables, or untried foods. Ordinarily, the conclusions are not formally thought out, and the individual may be quite unaware of having gone through any of the steps.

A third view of attitudes is that they are predispositions that have feeling, cognitive, and behavioral components (Wagner and Sherwood 1969). This means there is some knowledge (cognition) of the object of the attitude, an evaluation (feeling) of it, and some tendency or predisposition to act toward it (Rosenberg and Hovland 1960). When an attitude is simply expressed verbally without a response tendency, some researchers define that as *opinion* (Wagner and Sherwood 1969).

Attitudes include evaluations: Regardless of the specific conception or definition of attitudes, it is always assumed that they involve an evaluation, usually of liking or disliking, and that they influence what one does. However, since liking and disliking depend, in part, on a belief or knowledge about the object, changing beliefs or supplying information or knowledge will often change an attitude. For example, if we do not like a particular food but find that all our friends do, we may begin to believe that perhaps we are wrong and maybe the food has some good qualities. Subsequently, we may come to like it by convincing ourselves that the food tastes good— in which case our attitude is changed.

Methods of Changing Attitudes

Several methods have been used to bring about attitude change, but none has been universally successful. The specific methods proposed depend on the conception one has of attitudes and whether one thinks of them primarily as states of mind or as patterns of behavior. Lack of success in attitude change is due partly to using methods inappropriate to the attitude and to ignoring individual differences in the persons involved. A method that works for a weak attitude, an attitude held by a single individual, or one directed toward an object may not work for a strong attitude, one that is shared by a large group of people, or one directed toward other individuals.

Conceptions of Human Nature and Attitude Change

Conceptions of human nature play a role in selecting attitude-change techniques. If people are essentially nonthinking creatures of habit, a mechanistic conditioned-response approach should be effective. Simple learning techniques of pairing stimuli and responses could be employed. If humans are essentially perceptual by nature and if their behavior is a function of how they perceive the world, then efforts should be directed toward changing perceptions. If the perceptions are changed, the behavior emerging from those perceptions should take care of itself and change accordingly. Finally, if people are essentially rational and if their behavior depends on thinking and reasoning, logical arguments should move them to change their attitudes.

Each of these conceptions has its supporters among philosophers and psychologists, but probably no single conception is correct (Lyman 1985). Humans are at times rational or irrational, perceptual or machine-like, and they respond in different ways on different occasions. We may be swayed by reason when an attitude is weak, but resist all logic when it is strong. Or we may be shocked to discover that we have blindly acquired attitudes that contradict other beliefs or perceptual orientations.

Changing Attitudes by Changing Perceptions
Majority, Expert, and Prestige Opinion

The opinions of others are effective in changing beliefs, especially when we have no concrete or objective bases for the belief (Sherif 1935). It is common to speak of the effect of majority opinion, but for the majority opinion to hold sway, those who hold it, whether majority or experts, must have some prestige value. An adult's beliefs about the adverse effects of dietary fats and refined sugars would not be influenced by his or her children's contrary beliefs nor by the beliefs of a supposed expert who carried no respect. Because most humans have a need to belong and to be accepted by others, the majority opinion of peers strongly influences attitudes and beliefs, provided that certain conditions, as demonstrated in laboratory studies, are present.

The autokinetic effect: In studies using the autokinetic effect, a pinpoint of light is shown on the wall of a darkened room. The light does not move, but for almost all observers it appears to move or wander slowly for a short distance in an irregular fashion and direction. (*Autokinetic* means self-movement and refers to this apparent motion.) If a person is in the room with a number of others who say they see the light move in a particular direction, the person will also see the light move in that direction. The same effect occurs if a person who is considered to be an expert or who has other prestige value says the light moves in a given direction (Sherif 1935). However, if the light is made brighter and clearly visible or is surrounded by a frame of light, no movement is seen regardless of what the majority or the experts say. (The observer may *say* he sees the light move even though he or she does not.) The effect occurs only when the situation is ambiguous or unclear, and it depends on the absence of objective clues or criteria that the observer can use in making judgments of direction.

The opinions of others and changes in food preferences: With food, flavor takes the place of objective criteria. Majority, expert, or peer opinion that a food is good will bring about changes in preferences if the food is neutral or only mildly pleasant or unpleasant to the person. When the flavor is unclear or when the person is unsure of his or her feeling about the food or has no strong feeling about it, the situation is ambiguous, and individual attitudes can be altered by the opinions of others. If the food clearly tastes good or bad to the person, regardless of how it tastes to others or how others say it tastes, their opinions will have little or no effect on the person's attitude. However, the person might be pressured or induced by those opinions to try a food that he or she would otherwise refuse and may be more open-minded about considering its flavor qualities. Since trying a food is often the first step toward accepting and liking it, the opinions of others can affect preferences both directly and indirectly.

The opinions of others need not be expressed verbally. In fact, nonverbal communication through gestures, facial expressions, and the like is often more effective than verbal communication. When there is a difference of opinion between ourselves and others, we will pay more attention to what the others do than to what they say; in fact, we are on the alert for discrepancies between their words and their actions. Young children are particularly sensitive to gestures and facial expressions and to how things are said as opposed to what is said because they simply do not understand the words. The emotional meanings of the gestures and facial expressions are clearer to them than the semantic meanings of the words.

Rod-and-frame test: How independent are individuals in forming impressions and attitudes, particularly when situations are somewhat ambiguous? Do they rely on external cues, or are those ignored? Studies somewhat similar to the autokinetic-effect studies show that there are personality differences. In the rod-and-frame test (fig. 12-1), individuals in a dark room are shown a luminous rod within a luminous square frame. Both the rod and frame are tilted but their positions can be changed, and the observers are instructed to adjust the position of the rod so that it is vertical. Results show that some observers are strongly influenced in their

12–1. Some representative positions of the rod and frame in the rod-and-frame test

judgments by the position of the frame, making the rod parallel to the sides of the frame, while others ignore the position of the frame and make the rod upright in accordance with gravity (Witkin and Asch 1948). Relying on the position of the frame for judgment of the vertical is known as *field dependence,* in contrast with *field independence* in which the orientation of the frame is ignored (Witkin 1959). Other studies have shown that field-dependent individuals are more compliant and their attitudes are influenced by external cues including the opinions of others. Field-independent individuals are individualistic and rely more on their own standards and resources (Witkin and Berry 1975). Generally, adults are more field-independent than children, but there are wide variations among individuals.

The Perceptual Judgment Scale

In the course of our experience with objects, persons, events, and the like, we tend to build up a scale of values ranging from worst to best, most disliked to most liked, most undesirable to most desirable, and so on. This is known as a *perceptual judgment scale* (Sherif and Sherif 1956). As a result of seeing movies, we nonconsciously develop a conception of what constitutes good, average, and bad films; a film may be perceived as anything from thoroughly enjoyable to thoroughly unpleasant. Whenever we see a new film, we automatically place it somewhere along this scale of values from worst to best. If we have a somewhat unfavorable attitude toward films and think films are generally quite bad, that opinion can be improved by seeing a film that is slightly better than the film at the upper or favorable endpoint of the perceptual judgment scale. When this occurs, the scale of values is expanded beyond the endpoint, the new film is assimilated into the scale, and the general attitude toward films shifts in a positive direction. However, if the new film is extremely better than what we have until then considered to be the best film, the new film will be perceived as an exception, separate from all other films. The perceptual judgment scale then contracts, emphasizing the new film as a special case, and the opinion of films in general is worsened. The changes are shown schematically in figure 12-2.

In the course of our experience with foods, we build up similar evaluative judgment scales not only with respect to categories of foods such as meats and vegetables but also for individual foods. We have a fairly large number of such scales. They apply to every way in which foods can be classified: nutritiousness, tastiness, expensiveness; peasant, country, gourmet; dessert, breakfast, dinner; and so on.

Using the perceptual judgment scale to change food preferences: In using the perceptual judgment scale to change food likes and dislikes, the most effective approach is to modify the method of preparation and to use other

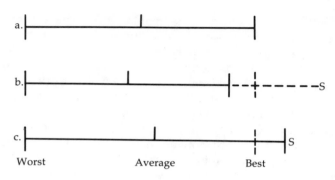

12–2. Schematic representation of the perceptual judgment scale (a) with a new stimulus (S) presented well beyond (b) and slightly beyond (c) the existing upper endpoint

techniques to change perceptions of the foods. The attitude toward vegetables can be improved by serving vegetables that are more carefully prepared and serving them in a more attractive manner. Usually there is less variation in the preparation of vegetables than of any other menu item. Too often they are simply boiled or baked with little added in the way of seasoning. Although that may be attractive to the purist, it is boring to others. Steamed green beans may be liked by some individuals for their flavor alone, but if they are not liked, and we want them to be, something must be done to pique interest and compensate for the lack of appealing flavor. A sprinkling of toasted almonds has become commonplace, but there are dozens of variations that will make the beans "taste" better than what one is accustomed to. In so doing, the judgment scale is expanded, and the attitude toward green beans becomes more favorable. If this approach is used with several vegetables, the opinion of vegetables as a class will be improved.

Many individuals do not like salt-free foods. This is due partly to their flavor, partly to their unfamiliarity, and perhaps most of all to the idea that one's diet is being restricted for reasons of health. Salt-free foods are thought of as being bland and tasteless, and, as usually served, they often are. The judicious use of herbs and spices quickly changes that and also changes attitudes toward salt-free foods. Once the attitude is even slightly changed, the negative response will be decreased and individuals will be less resistant to trying and eating salt-free foods. Since liking is partly a function of familiarity, simply getting people to eat those foods will strengthen the effect of the perceptual change and help to modify the attitude. Of course, common sense is essential. If highly disliked foods are served without salt, the negative attitude toward salt-free foods is strengthened. The judgment scale will take a giant leap in the negative direction, and all the positive changes will be undone.

Changing Attitudes Through Reason and Persuasion

Most of the research on attitude change comes from social rather than individual psychology and focuses on the use of reasoned arguments and persuasion to change the attitudes of groups or large numbers of people. Since groups are made up of individuals, the principles that apply to group change also apply to individual change.

The use of persuasion has four aspects: the persuader or communicator; the audience or target person to whom the message is directed and whose attitude one wishes to change; the message or communication itself; and the method of communication (Worchel and Cooper 1983).

The Communicator

Much of what has already been said about majority and expert opinion applies to the communicator. He or she must be—or give the appearance of being—trustworthy and must appear to have nothing to gain personally by changing the target person's attitude. Experts are more effective in changing beliefs when factual information is involved, but communicators who are similar to the target person are more effective in changing emotionally toned attitudes of liking and disliking (Goethals and Nelson 1973). An expert is more likely to convince an individual that a given food is healthy, but the target person's peers are more likely to convince him or her to eat the food because it tastes good.

Characteristics of the Target Person

Very little evidence exists to support the idea that there are general persuadable personalities, but a few personality traits are correlated with susceptibility to the opinions of others (Hovland and Janis 1959). The most important personal characteristics are the attitudes of the target person, the strength of those attitudes and the reasons for holding them, and the individual's interaction with the persuader and the message being communicated. The beliefs of those with low self-esteem are more easily changed than those of others who are more self-confident (Cohen 1959). As noted earlier, the attitudes of field-dependent individuals are also more susceptible to external influences.

The Message

How reasonable are people? Is it better to present the pros and cons of an argument on the assumption that logic will prevail and people will draw the correct conclusion? Or is it better to present only one side and run the risk of being called biased and having the opinion rejected for that reason? Studies show that presenting both sides of an argument is more effective if the individuals involved are opposed to the opinion or point of view being advocated (Hovland et al. 1949). Doing so tells the target persons they have reasonable grounds for the belief and lets them know they are not stupid for holding it. At the same time, it helps strengthen the idea that the persuader is reasonable and honest. This may be particularly important when adults deal with children. Presenting both sides, one of which supports the child's attitude, weakens what might otherwise be seen as parental authoritarianism. Presenting both sides is not necessarily an elaborate, complicated procedure. It may require only admitting the other point of view. With foods it may simply be a matter of conceding that "Yes, there are other vegetables that taste better, but carrots contain a lot of vitamin A which helps keep your eyes and skin healthy."

When the target person is already in favor of the opinion being advocated, presenting only arguments in favor of the position is most effective in strengthening it. Presenting a view already held enhances the target individual's ego by strengthening the sense of belonging and of being on the right side. If an attitude has been changed by hearing only one side, however, the attitude is less resistant to change by counterarguments later on (Lumsdaine and Janis 1953). Further, if the individual is aware that there is another side, presenting only one side may increase resistance to persuasion (Jones and Brehm 1970).

Method of Communication

Freedom to choose: It is often effective to present relevant information and let individuals draw their own conclusions, without telling them what the desired conclusion is. This makes them feel good about themselves for having arrived at the "right" conclusion on their own. It also fosters feelings of independence and forestalls feelings of being dominated by another or of giving in to another's will. This is desirable when feeling independent is important or when there is any indication of a power struggle, as there often is between children and adults or between those who know (or think they know) and those who do not. Real or imagined threats to freedom to behave or choose, as well as attempts by others to impose their wills produce resistance which makes forbidden acts more desirable (Brehm and Brehm 1981; Mazis 1982). As every parent knows, the increased attractiveness of forbidden acts results in greater determination to do what has been forbidden (Hammock and Brehm 1966) or in aggression against those who threaten freedom of choice (Worchel 1984).

Using emotions: Emotions play a role in changing attitudes. Putting the target person in a good mood, even when the mood is unrelated to the argument, increases acceptance of an argument and modifies attitudes (Biggers and Pryor 1982). A pleasant, friendly, and happy dinner table can help change attitudes toward foods. Generally, bad moods are not helpful. However, arguments that create fear in the target person can be effective in changing behavior if the person knows what to do to reduce the fear and if there is some equally attractive alternative behavior (Leventhal et al. 1965; Leventhal et al. 1967).

Nevertheless, the use of fear to change attitudes or behaviors is not a desirable procedure and should be used, if at all, only when really necessary and when all other methods have failed. It is doubtful that its use to change food preferences in children is ever justified. Eating and the social context in which it occurs are too important in the development of personality and interpersonal relations to jeopardize either of these by associating them with fear or other negative emotions.

Cognitive Dissonance

Whenever we have attitudes or beliefs that are inconsistent or incompatible with one another, or whenever we behave in ways inconsistent with our beliefs, there is mental conflict or discord known as *cognitive dissonance* (Festinger 1957). Tension develops, and we are motivated to modify our attitudes or change our behaviors in order to resolve the conflict and reduce the tension. Often the change is to justify the action or to maintain a favorable self-image. For example, if we believe that smoking is harmful but continue to smoke anyway, something has to give. Either we must confess that we smoke out of masochism or stupidity or we must justify our continued smoking by modifying our attitude. We might convince ourselves that smoking gives us needed relaxation, that safe cigarettes will be available before any harm is done, or that our addiction is so strong that quitting would cause aftereffects as bad as or worse than those caused by continued smoking.

Resolving dissonance: When dissonance arises from conflicting attitudes rather than from a conflict between an attitude and behavior, dissonance can be resolved by abandoning one of the attitudes. If we believe that acid rain should be stopped and also believe that industries producing acid rain should not be regulated, inconsistency will not exist if we give up one of the beliefs. It is also possible to resolve the conflict fairly well by keeping both beliefs but giving greater importance to one than to the other. Thus, one may believe that acid rain is a greater threat to the economy than regulation of industry. Both attitudes are retained, but dissonance disappears or is greatly reduced by giving a higher priority to one attitude over the other. An attitude can be strengthened also by bolstering it with additional arguments. If acid rain threatens the economy *and* endangers health, dissonance is decreased and regulation can be accepted. The conflict over disliking vegetables and knowing they are healthy can be resolved by recognizing that they are less expensive than other foods and that emphasizing them in a diet will also make us look better physically. The conflict could be resolved in favor of not eating them by believing we are already so healthy that they are not needed.

Resolving dissonance by changing behavior: When an attitude is inconsistent with behavior, the attitude is likely to change to justify or fit the behavior (Festinger and Carlsmith 1959). Rather than causing behavior, the new attitude is a result of it. This means that a desired change in attitude can be brought about if the person can be persuaded to engage in desired action. The reasons for this are not entirely clear, but it seems likely that by engaging in a given behavior the person makes, or believes he or she has made, a public commitment. Since the attitude is private and unknown, it is easier to shift the attitude than it is to renege on the behavior. This is especially true if the behavior has social approval and the attitude does not. When an attitude changes to fit behavior, the tendency to engage in that behavior is doubly strengthened, first, by the motivating attitude and, second, by the conditioning effect of engaging in the behavior.

Changing Food Preferences Through Dissonance

When we know a food is good for us but do not like it or refuse to eat it, or when we know a food is not healthful but like it and eat it anyway, dissonance is present. Our knowledge about the food is incompatible with our preferences and behaviors. Usually, the conflict is resolved by reference to the food's taste or flavor. Healthful foods do not "taste good," and sweet desserts are "so delicious." As discussed in chapter 2, this is a socially acceptable reason for eating or not eating specific foods and one that justifies actions and preserves self-esteem. Besides, it is also sometimes true!

Using dissonance theory, how can food preferences and eating patterns be changed? Since justifying actions makes it more difficult to change them, the most important first step is to avoid any kind of pressure or argument that requires or even suggests that the person must justify his or her preferences. Rationalizations and justifications can be found for anything, particularly when one is pushed. And once found, they as well as the original attitude and behavior must be changed. Of course, keeping silent at the proper time is often more easily said than done, especially when one's children seem to be eating all the wrong things. (One consolation is that since teenagers eat so much, they are likely to get most of the needed nutrients anyway.)

Creating dissonance: If coercion or the appearance of it is avoided, any of the methods for resolving dissonance could be used to help change food preferences. When dissonance does not exist and a change in food preferences is sought, it may be necessary to create dissonance so that the tension can be reduced by changing the attitude toward the food. If an individual does not like vegetables in the cabbage family and sees no reason to eat them, emphasizing their importance in the diet as a possible cancer preventative should create moderate dissonance: "I don't like them, but I should eat them." If the individual now tries the vegetables willingly or is induced to eat them either by persuasion or related techniques or by a new method of preparation and presentation, a more favorable attitude will develop. This is especially true if, as is often the case in food dislikes, their flavor is not actively disliked.

Usually, dissonance with respect to eating what we should not and not eating what we should already exists and needs no formal effort to create it. Purposely creating dissonance can have adverse effects on the person in whom it is created and on his or her relations with the person creating it. Since dissonance often involves guilt and other negative feelings, creating it in order to change attitudes should be done only when it is fairly certain that the dissonance will be resolved. Of course, when dissonance already exits, if it cannot be resolved entirely, even a partial resolution is psychologically desirable.

Individual *versus* Group Decisions
Discussion versus Lectures

The classic studies comparing the effectiveness of lectures *versus* discussions and of individual decisions *versus* group decisions in changing food habits were carried out in the early days of World War II (Lewin 1943). There was a shortage of meat at the time and attempts were being made to convince homemakers to use more of the cheaper, unfamiliar meats such as kidneys, brains, and hearts. Three groups of housewives were given lectures by a nutritionist who emphasized the health and nutritional values of the meats as well as the economic value of using them. Methods of preparation that would minimize the organ meats' unliked physical characteristics were discussed and recipes for preparing "delicious dishes" were distributed. Three comparable groups discussed the use of the meats. An experienced group leader led the discussion, and the nutritionist also participated. All groups then voted to try the meats. The results showed that the group-decision method clearly produced more change in food habits. A week after the decisions, 52 percent of those in the discussion groups had served at least one of the meats, while only 10 percent of those in the lecture groups had done so. Further, 23 percent of the women in the discussion groups and only 3 percent of those in the lecture groups served a food they had never served before.

It is clear that group discussion and decision produced greater changes in food habits than did a lecture by an expert, and the results are often cited as proof of the superiority of democratic discussion procedures. It is not clear, however, just how well the method would transfer to a family setting, where the atmosphere is much less formal and the parent is likely to be the expert and perhaps the discussion leader as well. The interplay between children and parents changes the meaning of those roles, and the situations are not comparable in other ways.

Discussions versus Requests

In another study, groups of college students living in dormitories were asked to discuss and decide on a proposal to eat more whole-wheat bread and less white bread. Other comparable groups were requested simply to change their eating habits. The results showed that the group-decision method resulted in a greater increase in whole-wheat-bread consumption. However, if the group majority favoring the increase was very small, the results were less favorable than those produced by the request method. Perhaps when a group decision is made by only a small majority, the other members of the group feel they are being coerced and resist the decision by behaving in opposition to it. Feelings of coercion can occur whether or not a majority is involved. Within the family, not all members are equal, and if a decision is favored by older, more powerful parents or brothers or sisters, a sense of coercion may be present and the decision may be opposed.

Changing Food Preferences Through Associations

The use of associations to change food preferences is shown by the following personal anecdote. A few years ago I made moussaka for dinner. It was a new dish that my children had never had before. My oldest and youngest sons seemed to enjoy it, but the middle son would not even taste it. At the time he was very interested in Greece and Greek mythology. I painted a picture of Greek farmers raising eggplant and tending sheep by the blue Aegean two thousand years ago and suggested they may have stopped their work to discuss the gods and eat this very dish under the shade of a twisted olive tree. He tried the dish, and it has been one of his favorites ever since. Now, moussaka has a distinctive flavor, and it is certainly not attractive, especially after it has been cut into. Further, eggplant and lamb rank quite low on most food-preferences lists. It seems reasonable to conclude that my son's willingness to try the moussaka and his liking for it as well were greatly influenced by the associations it was given.

The importance of associations in food meanings and preferences was stressed in chapter 11. Insofar as meanings and preferences depend on associations, changing associations or adding new ones will change meanings and food preferences.

Using associations to change food preferences offers two chances of success. Associations can affect both behaviors and attitudes. Changing attitudes toward food will certainly change responses to it, and cognitive dissonance suggests that changing behaviors will change underlying attitudes.

The major task is to identify the associations the food in question already has for the individual. If none is present, the problem is to establish appropriate positive ones. They can be general, like the visual associations of popularity, good looks, and financial well-being used in magazine and television advertisements for commercial products, but the more effective associations will have greater personal meaning and significance. That requires some knowledge of the individual and of his or her interests in order to evoke unique associations and to avoid the risk of suggesting associations with negative values. If a person is proud of being an independent thinker and does not like following the crowd, painting a picture of hundreds of people enjoying a food will ensure its continued rejection. Parents sometimes say, "Oh, I loved that when I was a child," but the child we are talking to is ready to rebel against anything done before the dawn of time, especially if it was the parents who did it.

Variety in associations: Some associations develop through direct experience with foods in specific settings or contexts. Foods eaten on a picnic become picnic foods and carry all those meanings of summer days and friendly informality. Sometimes, however, the same food has both pleasant and unpleasant associations. The fun of picnics may be tempered by recalling the unpleasant hassle of getting them organized. Picking wild blackberries or tending vegetables as a child might be pleasant recollections, but remembering having to weed the garden or recalling that the pasture with the blackberry patch is now a housing development are not. Thus, in shaping an attitude toward food, one needs to make a judicious selection of memories and associations that will evoke pleasant images and thoughts. Even nostalgia can be effective.

Images form chains or sequences in which one image triggers off a host of others. In the preceding chapter, lobster bisque was used to illustrate how associations with a particular food have complexity that goes far beyond what is directly experienced with the food. Thus, there are possibilities for arousing and establishing extremely varied associations for any given food. Among those are associations that can be used to change attitudes and food preferences.

CHAPTER 13

The Use of Food as Psychotherapy

Since foods have meanings and evoke complex associations composed of memories, feelings, emotions, attitudes, and beliefs involving pleasantness and unpleasantness, can they be used psychologically to alter emotions, moods, and outlooks, as well as to enhance the sense of well-being? Conversely, can they arouse negative feelings and moods of pessimism and depression? The answer from everyday experience is yes. That answer is also supported indirectly by several food-related studies.

Unlike many variables relevant to food preferences, emotions are not "fixed," as are cultural backgrounds or educational levels, for example. Nor are emotions an integral part of the personality like the self-concept, which is not easily changed. If preferences go with specific emotions, as was suggested in chapter 4, and if pleasant and unpleasant emotional associations go with specific foods, then serving specific foods should increase acceptance and have a salutary effect on moods and emotions.

Altering Emotions Through Foods

The use of foods to alter emotions and outlooks involves three separate but related questions. (1) What foods will evoke specific emotions? (2) What foods will strengthen, weaken, prolong, or terminate emotions already being experienced? (3) What foods will have an effect on the more general sense of well-being?

Although the following discussions are somewhat speculative because of the lack of extensive concrete data, if foods have psychologically therapeutic values, individual or group diet therapy could be initiated which uses the psychological as well as nutritional values of foods to modify moods and to foster psychological well-being. The foods served or selected could be used to guide and direct memories, recollections, and mental activities and contents. Choices could be made which would engender or enhance particular feelings, attitudes, and outlooks and would arouse pleasant memory associations while avoiding painful ones. Meals and snacks could offer a built-in "therapist" three or more times a day.

In view of the large number of consciously experienced emotions and the somewhat limited variety of physiological changes in emotions, especially in those that are weak or moderate, the psychological influences should be broader and more comprehensive in scope than nutritional-chemical intervention. Further, since emotion depends on experiential phenomena— images, ideas, thoughts, appraisals, and the like—all of which appear in food associations, individuals should be at least as sensitive and responsive, if not more so, to the emotional effects of associations as they are to the nutritional-chemical values of food.

Evoking Emotions

The use of foods to change emotions was discussed in chapter 4. The rationale is quite simple: through conditioning, foods eaten during specific emotions come to evoke those emotions in the future. If popcorn usually is eaten when one is feeling friendly, but not at other times, eating popcorn subsequently should tend to put the person in a friendly mood regardless of how he or she is feeling. Festive foods should put one in a festive mood, and foods associated with security and love should make one feel secure and loved. If peanut butter sandwiches usually are eaten when one is alone and lonely, they will evoke those feelings at other times. Because individuals share some of the same eating habits, there will be some similarity in the kinds of emotions evoked by specific foods. Mashed potatoes and gravy are not party foods and are unlikely to evoke feelings of conviviality. Soups often are served when one is not feeling well, but because they are given in a context of caring concern, they should evoke the security of feeling that someone cares, whether or not anyone else is present.

Modifying Existing Emotions

If an emotion is strengthened, prolonged, weakened, or terminated while food is eaten or shortly thereafter, that food should subsequently strengthen, weaken, prolong, or terminate the emotion. Again, this is simple conditioning or associative learning. A previously neutral stimulus (the food) present with a response (the emotional change) will tend to evoke that response whenever the stimulus is again present.

By combining the above procedure with the principles involved in arousing emotions, it should be possible to replace an existing emotion with one that is more desirable. If full meals of traditional roast beef and potatoes are preferred and eaten when one is feeling self-confident, full meals should enhance feelings of self-confidence on other occasions, including times when one is worried or anxious. Similarly, if wine prolongs feelings of love and affection, drinking wine should alter existing feelings of hostility; and foods that evoke or prolong feelings of friendliness should make one less lonely or jealous.

Identifying Food-Emotion Relations

In order to use foods effectively, individuals need to determine their own food-emotion relations. This is easily accomplished by keeping a record of the foods eaten during different emotions and recording their effects on the emotions. Since there is some evidence that individuals prefer what is best for them during different emotions (see chapter 4), a more systematic approach would be to begin with an emotion checklist that includes a variety of emotions or only those emotions one wishes to modify. Then, when a particular emotion is being experienced, the food items preferred should be identified, and one or another of them should be eaten. By eating only one food rather than several, its particular effect can be studied. The effect on the emotion should then be recorded, indicating whether the emotion was strengthened, weakened, prolonged, or terminated. It would make sense to record how one feels at intervals after having eaten the food: (1) immediately after (this effect would be more psychological than physiological), (2) thirty minutes or so later, when digestion is well under way, and (3) an hour or so later, when digestion and absorption of the food are in the final stages. This procedure would give information as to what foods modify what emotions. In order to discover whether or not there is a difference in the effectiveness of various foods, those not associated with changes in emotions could be eaten sometimes and the two results compared.

Enhancing Moods and the Sense of Well-being

Instead of specific foods acting directly on single emotions, foods may affect moods in more subtle ways. Single food items may arouse complex associations that have diffuse effects on moods and on one's general outlook or sense of well-being.

The emotion-food preference studies discussed in chapter 11 showed that there were more as well as different kinds of associations with liked foods than with disliked foods. Spontaneous comments from the respondents strongly suggested that these associations—the thoughts, ideas, and images—were related to food likes, dislikes, and acceptance. Individuals may dislike baked beans, not because of their taste but because they represent poverty. The importance of associations was supported also by observations made during a pilot study on food preferences at a care center for the elderly. One of the striking features seen at mealtime was the number of associations occurring with the patients' accepting or resisting the foods served. For example, vanilla pudding: "That's baby food, and I'm not a baby"; green peas: "We used to raise them in our garden"; meat loaf: "It must be Sunday leftovers"; frosted cake: "Whose birthday is it?" As in the studies with college students, the associations differed with respect to the kinds of references, and many of them involved memories and recollections.

With these kinds of complex associations, the images and thoughts fuse with feelings and emotions to form a complex whole that is characterized more by pleasantness or unpleasantness than by the occurrence of a single emotion. What is involved is an attitude or outlook, derived perhaps from a host of memories, in which leveling, sharpening, and assimilation have taken place. Some details are eliminated, others exaggerated, and still others added, thereby enhancing a principal theme. Images, although concrete and specific, contain within them meanings that go far beyond the actual visual scene. The image is an icon: it represents itself, but as a symbol it carries with it meaning and significance in which the concrete manifestation is relatively unimportant.

"We used to raise them in our garden" is a literal statement, but it emerges from a welter of thoughts, images, emotions, and ideas. To the speaker it symbolizes a complex mental content containing attitudes towards the "we" and "our," to the garden and to gardening, encompassing, perhaps, blue skies and summer rains. "To raise" captures meanings of growth and care, far different from "to have."

In contrast to simple conditioning, here the food is not a stimulus for evoking emotions directly. It is a symbol calling forth diverse associations that carry with them patterns of emotions, attitudes, ideas, and beliefs, characterized by an overall aura of pleasantness or unpleasantness. This air of pleasantness or unpleasantness, in conjunction with the specific associations, is particularly important in establishing moods and outlooks. Thus, the food is a symbol-stimulus for pleasant or unpleasant associations and for the moods or sense of well-being which they engender.

The implications of the above are that foods with positive or pleasant associations should lift depressed moods and enhance or perpetuate positive moods. If peas carry complex pleasant associations encompassing much more than a garden in the past, they should put one in a positive frame of mind. On the other hand, foods with negative associations should weaken or reverse pleasant moods or prolong existing negative ones. If foods in bland diets remind the elderly infirm of baby foods, they are likely to increase one's sense of dependent helplessness and to impair one's sense of well-being. If baked beans have unpleasant associations or connotations of being poor and broke, eating them while broke can only worsen one's depression. However, if they also have pleasant associations—the warmth of a loving family, or childhood poverty subsequently overcome—they might instill self-confidence and strengthen the belief that all will be well. With a positive outlook, the motivation and determination to deal with present adversity should be enhanced.

Preliminary Research

In order to test some of the above hypotheses, a preliminary study was carried out by the author. Forty university students were asked to keep a record of the foods actually eaten during twenty-two different emotions. They were asked to indicate also whether their emotions became weaker, stronger, or remained unchanged after eating and whether they felt better or worse psychologically. Four weeks after completing this part of the study, each student was given a list of the foods he or she had eaten and was asked to report the associations that came to mind when thinking of each food item and to indicate whether the associations were pleasant, unpleasant, or neutral in tone. This was done in order to determine the nature of the associations occurring with the various foods. The results were then analyzed to see if the pleasantness of the food associations had an effect on the emotions or moods being experienced when the foods were eaten.

Several practical problems prevent drawing clear conclusions from the study. (1) There was no control over the individuals' total diet; instead of eating foods with only pleasant or unpleasant associations, during the course of a day the individuals ate some foods with pleasant associations and others with unpleasant associations. (2) Nor did the foods eaten during a particular emotion consist of ones having *only* pleasant or unpleasant associations; often a given food had both kinds of associations. (3) During the period studied, the individuals experienced a much wider variety of emotions than those on the checklist and also ate many foods for which the pleasantness of the associations was not identified. (4) In order to affect the *general* sense of well-being, a diet consisting of only those foods with pleasant or unpleasant associations would need to be maintained for a period of several weeks.

Results: In spite of the shortcomings of the study, there are several points of interest. Overall, approximately two-thirds of the individuals reported feeling better after eating. This confirms the common belief that eating makes one happier. However, the effect varied with the initial mood as well as with the pleasantness of the associations. Ninety-seven percent of those already in a positive mood felt better after eating foods with pleasant associations, while only 64 percent of those in an initial negative mood felt better. Of those eating foods with unpleasant associations, only 38 percent of those in a negative mood felt better afterwards, and 60 percent felt worse. If the initial emotion was positive, 24 percent felt worse. Generally, the results suggest that associations enhance existing moods. If the initial mood is positive, individuals will feel better if the associations are pleasant. If the initial mood is negative, they will feel worse if the associations are unpleasant.

Implications: The results make it clear that the pleasantness of food associations affects emotions. Further research is justified, and it seems reasonable that a more precise study, in which the foods eaten and the values of the associations were more clearly identified and carefully controlled, might show that associations can actually reverse existing moods and emotions.

An easily controlled but logistically difficult study is suggested in order to determine the effect of the pleasantness of associations on the general long-term sense of well-being. The first step would be to identify the values of the associations a number of individuals have with a large number of foods and then allow them to eat only those foods with pleasant associations and require them to avoid all foods having neutral or unpleasant associations. It would also be necessary to ensure that the individuals had a balanced, healthful diet. If the persons' scores on a sense-of-well-being test went up after several weeks but did not change or became worse for similar individuals eating foods with neutral or unpleasant associations, it would be reasonable to conclude that food with pleasant associations was having a therapeutic effect. A similar study should be carried out to determine the effects of negative associations.

Evaluation of the Food-Mood Relation

The use of food as psychotherapy is reasonable and logically based on psychological principles and what we know about emotions, associations, conditioning, and associative learning. But what is reasonable is not always true, and the idea seemed eccentric when first considered. However, the results from the preliminary research cited above lend support to the hypothesis. Additional research is needed not only on the therapeutic effects of food's association values, but also on how these might work in conjunction with the chemical effects of various food substances.

CHAPTER 14

Conclusion

In *Four Quartets* T. S. Eliot says that the goal of all our searching is to end up where we started and to understand it for the first time. It is hoped that the material in this book has contributed toward a psychology of food and our understanding of food preferences: why we prefer some foods and dislike others, why some preferences fluctuate from day to day while others remain constant, how preferences develop and change, and the effects of preferences on our emotional life and sense of well-being.

Possible answers to these questions have been suggested. The approach has been psychological, but the topic is extremely broad and much remains unknown. There are often conflicting data and theories, stemming not only from differences in research methods and procedures but also from differences in philosophical assumptions and conceptions. Further, psychologists have neglected some of the practical problems of interest to nutritionists and foodservice personnel. Food-texture perception and the role of form and color in food acceptance and preference are some examples. Nevertheless, facts from psychological research and principles from general psychology apply quite well to food psychology. More research specifically designed to answer questions of theory and practice should contribute further to the field.

BIBLIOGRAPHY

Ahsen, A. 1986. The new structuralism: Images in dramatic interlock. *Journal of Mental Imagery*, 10(3): 1–92.

Amendola, J. 1969. *Ice carving made easy* (5th rev. ed.) New Haven: Culinary Institute of America.

Amoore, J. E. 1970. *Molecular basis of odor*. Springfield, Ill.: Thomas.

Arnold, M. 1984. Imagery and psychophysical response. *Journal of Mental Imagery*, 8(4): 43–50.

Asch, S. 1946. Forming impressions of personality. *Journal of Abnormal and Social Psychology*, 41: 258–90.

Asch, S. 1952. *Social psychology*. Englewood Cliffs, N.J.: Prentice-Hall.

Asch, S. E. See Witkin and Asch.

Back, K. W., and Glasgow, M. 1981. Social networks and psychological condition in diet preferences: Gourmets and vegetarians. *Basic and Applied Social Psychology*, 2: 1–9.

Baker, A. H.; Rierdan, J; and Napner, S. 1974. Age changes in size-value phenomena. *Child Development*, 45: 257–68.

Bandura, A. 1977. *Social learning theory*. Englewood Cliffs, N. J.: Prentice-Hall.

Barker, L. M., ed. 1982. *The psychobiology of human food selection*. Westport, Conn.: AVI.

Bartlett, F. 1932. *Remembering*. Cambridge: Cambridge University Press.

Bartley, S. H. 1958. *Principles of perception*. New York: Harper Brothers.

Bartoshuk, L. 1980 (September). Separate worlds of taste. *Psychology Today*, 14(4): 48–57.

Bartoshuk, L. 1981. The chemical senses. In J. W. Kling and L. A. Riggs, eds., *Woodworth & Schlosberg's experimental psychology* (3rd ed.). New York: Holt, Rinehart & Winston.

Bartsch, D. See Klesges, Bartsch, Norwood, Kautzman, and Haugrud.

Bass, M. A.; Wakefield, L.; and Kolassa, K. 1979. *Community nutrition and individual food behavior*. Minneapolis: Burgess.

Bate-Smith, E. C. See Harper, Bate-Smith, and Land; Harper, Land, Griffiths, and Bate-Smith.

Baum, A.; Singer, J. E.; and Valins, S.; eds. 1978. *Advances in environmental psychology*. Hillsdale, N.J.: Erlbaum.

Beatty, W. W. See Berry, Beatty, and Klesges.

Beets, M.G.J. 1978. Odor and stimulant structure. In E. C. Carterette and M. P. Friedman, eds., *Handbook of perception, VIA*. New York: Academic Press.

Beidler, L. M. 1966. Chemical excitation of taste and odor receptors. In I. Hornstein, ed., *Flavor chemistry*. Washington, D.C.: American Chemical Society.

Beidler, L. M. 1978. Biophysics and chemistry of taste. In E. C. Carterette & M. P. Friedman, eds., *Handbook of perception, VIA*. New York: Academic Press.

Beidler, L. M. 1983. Biological basis of food selection. In L. M. Barker, ed., *Human food selection*. Westport, Conn.: AVI.

Bennett, C. 1977. *Spaces for people*. Englewood Cliffs, N.J.: Prentice-Hall.

Berlyne, D. 1971. *Aesthetics and psychobiology*. New York: Appleton-Century-Crofts.

Berry, J. W. See Witkin and Berry.

Berry, S. L.; Beatty, W. W.; and Klesges, R. C. 1985. Sensory and social influences on ice-cream consumption by males and females in a lab setting. *Appetite*, 6: 41–45.

Bevan, W. See Dukes and Bevan.

Biggers, T., and Pryor, B. 1982. Attitude change: A function of emotion-eliciting qualities of environment. *Personality and Social Psychology Bulletin*, 8: 94–99.

Birch, D. See Birch, Birch, Marlin, and Kramer.

Birch, L. L. 1979a. Dimensions of preschool children's food preferences. *Journal of Nutrition Education*, 11: 77–80.

Birch, L. L. 1979b. Preschool children's food preferences and consumption patterns. *Journal of Nutrition Education*, 11: 189–92.

Birch, L. L. 1980a. The relationship between children's food preferences and those of their parents. *Journal of Nutrition Education*, 12: 14–18.

Birch, L. L. 1980b. Effects of peer models' food choices and eating behaviors on preschoolers' food preferences. *Child Development*, 51: 489–96.

Birch, L. L. 1981. A call for the explicit recognition of affect in models of human eating behavior. *Journal of Nutrition Education*, 13(1): S49–S53.

Birch, L. L.; Birch, D.; Marlin, D.; and Kramer, L. 1982. Effects of instrumental eating on children's food preferences. *Appetite*, 3: 125–34.

Birch, L. L., and Marlin, D. W. 1982. I don't like it; I never tried it; effect of exposure on two-year-old children's food preferences. *Appetite*, 3: 353–60.

Birch, L. L.; Marlin, D. W.; and Rotter, J. 1984. Eating as the "means" activity in a contingency: Effects on young children's food preference. *Child Development*, 55: 431–39.

Birch, L. L.; Zimmerman, S. I.; and Hind, H. 1980. The influence of social-affective context on the formation of children's food preferences. *Child Development*, 51: 856–61.

Birren, F. 1969. *Light, color, and environment*. New York: Van Nostrand Reinhold.

Blackman, S. L.; Singer, R. D.; and Mertz, T. 1983. The effects of social setting, perceived weight category, and gender on eating behavior. *Journal of Psychology*, 114: 115–22.

Blumer, H. 1968. Fashion. In *The international encyclopedia of the social sciences*. New York: Macmillan.

Boudreau, J. C. 1979. The taste of foods. In J. C. Boudreau, ed., *Food taste chemistry*. Washington, D.C.: American Chemical Society.

Bourne, M. C. 1966. A classification of objective methods for measuring texture and consistency of foods. *Journal of Food Science*, 31: 1011–14.

Bourne, M. C. 1978. Texture profile analysis. *Food Technology*, 22: 62–72.

Bourne, M. C. 1982. *Food texture and viscosity: Concept and measurement*. New York: Academic Press.

Brecher, A. See Cheraskin, Ringsdove, and Brecher.

Brehm, J. W. See Brehm and Brehm; Hammock and Brehm; Jones and Brehm.

Brehm, S. S., and Brehm, J. W. 1981. *Psychological reactance: A theory of freedom and control*. New York: Academic Press.

Brown, R. 1965. *Social psychology*. New York: The Free Press.

Bruner, J. S., and Goodman, C. C. 1947. Value and need as organizing factors in perception. *Journal of Abnormal and Social Psychology*, 42: 33–44.

Buckalew, L. W. See Sallis and Buckalew.

Cabanac, M. 1971. Physiological role of pleasure. *Science*, 173: 1103–7.

Cabanac, M. See also Duclaux, Feisthauer, and Cabanac.

Cain, W. S. 1978a. History of research on smell. In E. C. Carterette and M. P. Friedman, eds., *Handbook of perception, VIA*. New York: Academic Press.

Cain, W. S. 1978b. The odoriferous environment and the application of olfactory research. In E. C. Carterette and M. P. Friedman, eds., *Handbook of perception, VIA*. New York: Academic Press.

Cain, W. S. 1979. To know with the nose: Keys to odor identification. *Science*, 203: 467–69.

Cannon, W. B. 1939. *The wisdom of the body* (2nd ed.). New York: Norton.

Carlsmith, J. M. See Festinger and Carlsmith.

Charley, H. 1982. *Food science* (2nd ed.). New York: Wiley.

Cheraskin, E.; Ringsdove, W. M., Jr.; and Brecher, A. 1976. *Psychodietetics*. New York: Bantam.

Cherry, J. P., ed. 1981. *Protein functionality in foods*. Washington, D.C.: American Chemical Society.

Child, J. 1978. *Julia Child and company*. New York: Knopf.

Christensen, C. M. 1984. Food texture perception. In C. O. Chichester, E. M. Mrak, and B. S. Schweigert, eds., *Advances in food research*, vol. 29. New York: Academic Press.

Christensen, C. M., and Navazesh, M. 1984. Anticipatory salivary flow to the sight of different foods. *Appetite*, 5: 307–15.

Christman, R. J. 1971. *Sensory experience* (2nd ed.). New York: Harper & Row.

Cinciripini, P. M. 1984. Food choice and eating behavior among obese, lean, and normal individuals. *Behavior Modification*, 8: 425–43.

CKO News 1985 (November 6). Vancouver, B.C.

Cohen, A. R. 1959. Some implications of self-esteem for social influence. In C. I. Hovland and I. L. Janis, eds., *Personality and persuasibility*. New Haven: Yale University Press.

Coleman, P. H. See Krondl, Lay, Yurkin, and Coleman.

Collings, V. B. See McBurney, Collings, and Glanz.

Consumer Reports 1986 (September). Where does all the money go? Vol. 51(9): 581–92.

Cooper, J. See Worchel and Cooper.

Cowart, B. J. 1981. Development of taste perception in humans: Sensitivity and preference throughout the life span. *Psychological Bulletin*, 90: 47–73.

Crocker, E. C. 1945. *Flavor*. New York: McGraw-Hill.

Crutchfield, R. S. See Krech and Crutchfield.

Daniel, W. W. 1978. *Applied nonparametric statistics*. Boston: Houghton Mifflin.

Davis, C. M. 1928. Self-selection of diet by newly weaned infants. *American Journal of Diseases of Children*, 36: 651–79.

Davis, H. See Stevens and Davis.

Dember, W. N., and Warm, J. S. 1979. *Psychology of perception* (3rd ed.). New York: Holt, Rinehart & Winston.

Desor, J. A.; Maller, O; and Turner, R. E. 1973. Taste in acceptance of sugars in human infants. *Journal of Comparative and Physiological Psychology*, 84: 496–501.

Donnenwerth, G. V. See Kish and Donnenwerth.

Douglas, M. 1979 (July). Accounting for taste. *Psychology Today*, 13(7):44–51.

Dubbert, P. M.; Johnson, W. G.; Schlundt, D. G.; and Montague, N. 1984. The influence of caloric information on cafeteria food choices. *Journal of Applied Behavior Analysis*, 17: 85–92.

Duclaux, R.; Feisthauer, J.; and Cabanac, M. 1973. Effects of eating a meal on the pleasantness of food and non-food odors in man. *Physiology and Behavior*, 10: 1029–33.

Dufty, W. 1975. *Sugar Blues*. New York: Warner.

Dukes, W. F., and Bevan, W. 1952. Accentuation and response variability in the perception of relevant objects. *Journal of Personality*, 20: 457–65.

Einstein, M. A., and Hornstein, I. 1970. Food preferences of college students and nutritional implications. *Journal of Food Science*, 35: 429–35.

Engen, T. 1982. *The perception of odors*. New York: Academic Press.

Erickson, R. P. See Schiffman and Erickson.

Escalona, S. K. 1945. Feeding disturbances in very young children. *American Journal of Orthopsychiatry*, 15: 76–80.

Eysenck, M. D. 1944. An experimental and statistical study of olfactory preferences. *Journal of Experimental Psychology*, 34: 246–51.

Fallon, A. See Rozin and Fallon; Rozin, Fallon, and Mandell.

Fallon, A. E.; Rozin, P.; and Pliner, P. 1984. The child's concept of food: The development of food rejections with special reference to disgust and contamination sensitivity. *Child Development*, 55: 566–75.

Family Economics Review 1986. No. 3: 8.

Fantz, R. L. 1966. Pattern discrimination and selective attention as determinants of perceptual development from birth. In A. H. Kidd and J. F. Rivoire, eds., *Perceptual development in children*. New York: International Universities Press.

Feisthauer, J. See Duclaux, Feisthauer, and Cabanac.

Festinger, L. 1957. *A theory of cognitive dissonance*. Stanford, Calif.: Stanford University Press.

Festinger, L., and Carlsmith, J. M. 1959. Cognitive consequences of forced compliance. *Journal of Abnormal and Social Psychology*, 58: 203–10.

Fleck, H. 1981. *Introduction to nutrition* (3rd ed.). New York: Macmillan.

Fox, D. T. See Jeffrey, McLellarn, and Fox.

Freedman, J. 1975. *Crowding and behavior*. San Francisco: Freeman.

Galler, J. R., ed. 1984. *Nutrition and behavior*. New York: Plenum.

Garb, J. L., and Stunkard, A. J. 1974. Taste aversions in man. *American Journal of Psychiatry*, 131: 1204–7.

Gent, J. F. See McBurney and Gent.

George, R. S., and Krondl, M. 1983. Perceptions and food use of adolescent boys and girls. *Nutrition and Behavior*, 1: 115–25.

Gibson, J. J. 1966. *The senses considered as perceptual systems*. Boston: Houghton Mifflin.

Gibson, W. See Goldberg, Gorn, and Gibson.

Gifft, H. H.; Washbon, M. B.; and Harrison, C. G. 1976. *Nutrition, behavior and change*. Englewood Cliffs, N.J.: Prentice-Hall.

Glanz, L. M. See McBurney, Collings, and Glanz.

Glasgow, M. See Back and Glasgow.

Gleitman, H. 1981. *Psychology*. New York: Norton.

Goethals, G. R., and Nelson, R. E. 1973. Similarity in the influence process: The belief-value dimension. *Journal of Personality and Social Psychology*, 25: 117–22.

Goldberg, M. E.; Gorn, G. J.; and Gibson, W. 1978. TV messages for snack and breakfast foods: Do they influence children's preferences? *Journal of Consumer Research*, 5: 73–80.

Goldstein, K., and Sheerer, M. 1941. Abstract and concrete behavior. An experimental study with special tests. *Psychological Monographs*, 53 (no. 239).

Goodman, C. C. See Bruner and Goodman.

Gorn, G. J. See Goldberg, Gorn, and Gibson.

Griffiths, J. M. See Harper, Land, Griffiths, and Bate-Smith.

Grotkowski, M. L., and Sims, L. S. 1978. Nutritional knowledge, attitudes, and dietary practices of the elderly. *Journal of the American Dietetic Association*, 72: 499–506.

Gruss, L. P. See Kissileff, Gruss, Thornton, and Jordan.

Guilford, J. P. 1934. The affective value of color as a function of hue, tint, and chroma. *Journal of Experimental Psychology*, 17, 342–70.

Gunary, R. See Rolls, Rowe, Rolls, Kingston, Megson, and Gunary.

Hainer, R. M.; Emslie, A. G.; and Jacobson, A. 1954. An information theory of olfaction. *Annals of the New York Academy of Science*, 58: 158–74.

Hammock, T., and Brehm, J. W. 1966. The attractiveness of choice alternatives when freedom to choose is eliminated by a social agent. *Journal of Personality*, 34: 546–54.

Harper, R.; Bate-Smith, E. C.; and Land, D. G. 1968. *Odour description and odour classification: A multidisciplinary examination*. New York: American Elsevier.

Harper, R.; Land, D. G.; Griffiths, N. M.; & Bate-Smith, E. C. 1968. Odour qualities: A glossary of usage. *British Journal of Psychology*, 59: 231–52.

Harriman, A. E. See Ross and Harriman.

Harrison, C. G. See Gifft, Washbon, and Harrison.

Hatlelid, D. See Lyman, Hatlelid, and Macurdy.

Haugrud, S. See Klesges, Bartsch, Norwood, Kautzman, and Haugrud.

Hawkins, D. See Pauling and Hawkins.

Hazzard, F. W. 1930. A descriptive account of odors. *Journal of Experimental Psychology*, 13(4): 297–331.

Hertzler, A. A. 1983. Children's food patterns—a review: 1. Food preferences and feeding problems. *Journal of the American Dietetic Association*, 83(5): 551–54.

Hevner, K. 1935. Experimental studies of the affective value of colors and lines. *Journal of Applied Psychology*, 19: 385–98.

Hind, H. See Birch, Zimmerman, and Hind.

Honkavaara, S. 1958. A critical reevaluation of the color and form reaction, and disproving of the hypothesis connected with it. *Journal of Psychology*, 45: 25–36.

Hornstein, I. See Einstein and Hornstein.

Hovland, C. I., and Janis, I. L., 1959. *Personality and persuasibility*. New Haven: Yale University Press.

Hovland, C. I.; Lumsdaine, A.; and Sheffield, F. 1949. *Experiments on mass communications*. Princeton, N.J.: Princeton University Press.

Hovland, C. I. See also Rosenberg and Hovland.

Institutions 1979 (March 1). Vol. 84(5): 69–72.

Jacobs, K. W., and Nordan, F. M. 1979. Classification of placebo drugs: Effect of color. *Perceptual and Motor Skills*, 49: 367–72.

Jacobson, M. F. 1975. *Nutrition Scoreboard*. New York: Avon.

Janis, I. See Lumsdaine and Janis.

Jeffrey, D. B.; McLellarn, R. W.; and Fox, D. T. 1982. The development of children's eating habits: The role of television commercials. *Health Education Quarterly*, 9:174–89.

Jerome, N. W. See Kandel, Jerome, and Pelto.

Johnson, W. G. See Dubbert, Johnson, Schlundt, and Montague.

Jones, R. A., and Brehm, J. W. 1970. Persuasiveness of one- and two-sided communications as a function of awareness there are two sides. *Journal of Experimental Social Psychology*, 6: 47–56.

Jones, S. See Leventhal, Singer, and Jones.

Jordan, H. A. See Kissileff, Gruss, Thornton, and Jordan.

Jowitt, R. 1974. The terminology of food texture. *Journal of Texture Studies*, 5:351–58.

Judd, D. B., and Kelly, K. L. 1939. Method of designating colors. National Bureau of Standards. *Journal of Research*, 23: 355–85.

Kahn, E. L. See Szczesniak and Kahn.

Kalmus, H. 1952. Inherited sense defects. *Scientific American*, 186(5): 64–70.

Kamen, J. M., and Peryam, D. R. 1961. Acceptability of repetitive diets. *Food Technology*, 15: 173–77.

Kamen, J. M. See also Pilgrim and Kamen.

Kandel, R. F.; Jerome, N. W.; and Pelto, G. H. 1980. Contemporary approaches to diet and culture—Introduction. In R. F. Kandel, N. W. Jerome, and G. H. Pelto, eds., *Nutritional Anthropology*.

Karl, R. V. 1974. Familiarity and attraction to stimuli: Developmental change or methodological artifact? *Journal of Experimental Child Psychology*, 18: 504.

Katz, D. 1935. *The world of colour* (trans. by R. B. MacLeod and C. W. Fox). London: Paul.

Katz, S. H. 1982. Food, behavior, and biocultural evolution. In L. M. Barker, ed., *The psychophysiology of human food selection*. Westport, Conn.: AVI.

Kautzman, D. See Klesges, Bartsch, Norwood, Kautzman, and Haugrud.

Keinonen, M. See Prattala and Keinonen.

Keith, D. J. See Schafer and Keith.

Kelly, K. L. See Judd and Kelly.

Kenshalo, D. R. 1971. The cutaneous senses. In J. W. Kling and L. A. Riggs, eds., *Woodworth and Schlosberg's experimental psychology* (3rd ed.). New York: Holt, Rinehart & Winston.

Kenshalo, D. R. 1977. Age changes in touch, vibration, temperature, kinesthesis, and pain sensitivity. In J. E. Birren and K. W. Schaie, eds., *Handbook of the psychology of aging*. New York: Van Nostrand Reinhold.

King, S. 1980. Presentation and the choice of food. In M. Turner, ed., *Nutrition and lifestyles*. London: Applied Science Publishing.

Kingston, B. See Rolls, Rowe, Rolls, Kingston, Megson, and Gunary.

Kish, G. B., and Donnenwerth, G. V. 1972. Sex differences in the correlates of stimulus seeking. *Journal of Consulting and Clinical Psychology*, 38: 42–49.

Kissileff, H. R.; Gruss, L. P.; Thornton, J.; and Jordan, H. A. 1984. The satiating efficiency of foods. *Physiology and Behavior*, 32: 319–32.

Klesges, R. C.; Bartsch, D.; Norwood, J. D.; Kautzman, D.; and Haugrud, S. 1983. The effects of selected social and environmental variables on the eating behavior of adults in the natural environment. *International Journal of Eating Disorders*, 3: 35–41.

Klesges, R. C. See also Berry, Beatty, and Klesges.

Kling, J. W., and Riggs, L. A. 1971. *Woodworth and Schlosberg's experimental psychology* (3rd ed.). New York: Holt, Rinehart & Winston.

Kolassa, K. See Bass, Wakefield, and Kolassa.

Kramer, A. 1973. Food texture—Definition, measurement and relation to other food-quality attributes. In A. Kramer & A. S. Szczesniak, eds., *Texture measurements of foods*. Dordrecht, Holland: D. Reidel.

Kramer, L. See Birch, Birch, Marlin, and Kramer.

Krantz, D. S. 1979. A naturalistic study of social influences on meal size among moderately obese and nonobese subjects. *Psychosomatic Medicine*, 41: 19–27.

Krech, D., and Crutchfield, R. S. 1958. *Elements of psychology*. New York: Knopf.

Kretchmer, N. 1978. Lactose and lactase. In N. Kretchmer, ed., *Human nutrition: Readings from Scientific American*. San Francisco: Freeman.

Krondl, M.; Lay, D.; Yurkin, M. A.; and Coleman, P. H. 1982. Food use and perceived food meanings of the elderly. *Journal of the American Dietetic Association*, 80: 523–29.

Kupchella, C. 1976. *Sights and sounds*. Indianapolis: Bobbs-Merrill.

Land, D. G. See Harper, Land, Griffiths, and Bate-Smith; Harper, Bate-Smith, and Land.

Lay, D. See Krondl, Lay, Yurkin, and Coleman.

Leijonhielm, C. 1967. *Colours, forms and art*. Stockholm: Almquist & Wiksell.

LeMagnen, J. See Pierson and LeMagnen.

Leventhal, H.; Singer, R.; and Jones, S. 1965. The effects of fear and specificity of recommendation in persuasive communication. *Journal of Personality and Social Psychology*, 2: 20–29.

Leventhal, H.; Watts, J. C.; and Pagano, F. 1967. Effects of fear and instructions on how to cope with danger. *Journal of Personality and Social Psychology*, 6: 313–21.

Lewin, K. 1943. Forces behind food habits and methods of change. *Bulletin of the National Research Council*, 108: 35–65.

Loew, B. J. See Szczesniak, Loew, and Skinner.

Logue, A. W. 1986. *The psychology of eating and drinking.* New York: W. H. Freeman.

Lumsdaine, A., and Janis, I. 1953. Resistance to "counter-propaganda" produced by one-sided and two-sided "propaganda" presentations. *Public Opinion Quarterly,* 17: 311–18.

Lundholm, H. 1921. The affective tone of lines. *Psychological Review,* 28: 43–60.

Lyman, B. 1979. Representation of complex emotional and abstract meanings by simple forms. *Perceptual and Motor Skills,* 49: 839–42.

Lyman, B. 1982a. Menu item preferences and emotions. *School Food Service Research Review,* 6(1): 32–35.

Lyman, B. 1982b. The nutritional values and food group characteristics of foods preferred during various emotions. *Journal of Psychology,* 112: 121–27.

Lyman, B. 1984. An experiential theory of emotion. *Journal of Mental Imagery,* 8(4): 77–86.

Lyman, B. 1985. *Recurring problems in psychology* (rev. ed.). Vancouver, B. C.: Leopold Berger.

Lyman, B.; Hatlelid, D.; and Macurdy, C. 1981. Stimulus-person cues in first-impression attraction. *Perceptual and Motor Skills,* 52: 59–66.

Lyman, B., and Waters, J.C.E. 1986. The experiential loci and sensory qualities of various emotions. *Motivation and Emotion,* 10: 25–37.

Lyman, B., and Waters, J.C.E. (in press). Patterns of imagery in various emotions. *Journal of Mental Imagery.*

Macurdy, C. See Lyman, Hatlelid, and Macurdy.

Mahlamaki-Kultanen, S. See Tuorila-Ollikainen and Mahlamaki-Kultanen.

Mandell, R. See Rozin, Fallon, and Mandell.

Marlin, D. W. See Birch, Birch, Marlin, and Kramer; Birch and Marlin; Birch, Marlin, and Rotter.

Matlin, M. W. 1983. *Perception.* Boston: Allyn and Bacon.

Mazis, M. B. 1982. Antipollution measures and psychological reactance theory: A field experiment. *Journal of Personality and Social Psychology,* 42: 303–13.

McBurney, D. H. 1978. Psychological dimensions and perceptual analyses of taste. In E. C. Carterette and M. P. Friedman, eds., *Handbook of perception, VIA.* New York: Academic Press.

McBurney, D. H.; Collings, V. B.; and Glanz, L. M. 1973. Temperature dependence of human taste responses. *Physiology and Behavior,* 11: 89–94.

McBurney, D. H., and Gent, J. F. 1979. On the nature of taste qualities. *Psychological Bulletin,* 86: 151–67.

McLellarn, R. W. See Jeffrey, McLellarn, and Fox.

Megson, A. See Rolls, Rowe, Rolls, Kingston, Megson, and Gunary.

Meiselman, H. L., and Waterman, D. 1978. Food preferences of enlisted personnel in the armed forces. *Journal of the American Dietetic Association,* 73: 621–29.

Meiselman, H. L. See also Wyant and Meiselman.

Merleau-Ponty, M. 1962. *Phenomenology of perception* (trans. by C. Smith). London: Routledge & Kegan Paul.

Mertz, T. See Blackman, Singer, and Mertz.

Miller, D. L. 1985. *Introduction to collective behavior.* Belmont, Cal.: Wadsworth.

Miller, G. A. 1956. The magic number seven, plus or minus two. *Psychological Review,* 63: 81–97.

Miller, S. A., ed. 1981. *Nutrition and behavior*. Philadelphia: Franklin Institute.

Moncrieff, R. W. 1966a. Changes in olfactory preferences with age. *Revue de Laryngologie Otologie Rhinologie*, 86: 895–904.

Moncrieff, R. W. 1966b. *Odour preferences*. New York: Wiley.

Montagne, P. 1961. *Larousse gastronomique*. (ed. by N. Froud and C. Turgeon). London: Hamlyn.

Montague, N. See Dubbert, Johnson, Schlundt, and Montague.

Moskowitz, H. R. 1978a. Taste and food technology: Acceptability, aesthetics, and preference. In E. C. Carterette and M. P. Friedman, eds., *Handbook of perception. VIA*. New York: Academic Press.

Moskowitz, H. R. 1978b. Food and food technology: Food habits, gastronomy, flavors, and sensory evaluation. In E. C. Carterette and M. P. Friedman, eds., *Handbook of Perception, VIA*. New York: Academic Press.

Mozell, M. M. 1971. The chemical senses: II. Olfaction. In J. W. Kling and L. A. Riggs, eds., *Woodworth and Schlosberg's experimental psychology* (3rd ed.). New York: Holt, Rinehart & Winston.

Mueller, C. G. 1965. *Sensory psychology*. Englewood Cliffs, N.J.: Prentice-Hall.

Murch, G. M. 1973. *Visual and auditory perception*. Indianapolis: Bobbs-Merrill.

Murch, G. M. 1976. *Studies in perception*. Indianapolis: Bobbs-Merrill.

Napner, S. See Baker, Rierdan, and Napner.

Navazesh, M. See Christensen and Navazesh.

Neff, W. S. 1985. *Psychology of work and behavior* (3rd ed.). New York: Aldine.

Nelson, R. E. See Goethals and Nelson.

Nieman, C. 1961. *Colors recently authorised in 43 countries*. Amsterdam.

Nordan, F. M. See Jacobs and Nordan.

Norwood, J. D. See Klesges, Bartsch, Norwood, Kautzman, and Haugrud.

Osgood, C. E. 1952. The nature and measurement of meaning. *Psychological Bulletin*, 49: 197–237.

Otis, L. P. 1984. Factors influencing the willingness to taste unusual foods. *Psychological Reports*, 54: 739–45.

Pagano, F. See Leventhal, Watts, and Pagano.

Pangborn, R. M. 1984. Sensory techniques of food analysis. In D. W. Gruenwedel and J. R. Whitaker, eds., *Food analysis: Principles and techniques*, vol. 1. New York: Marcel Dekker.

Paul, B., ed., 1955. *Health, culture and community*. New York: Russell Sage Foundation.

Pauling, L., and Hawkins, D., eds., 1980. *Orthomolecular psychiatry*. San Francisco: W. H. Freeman.

Pearson, L. R. See Pearson and Pearson.

Pearson, L., and Pearson, L. R. 1976. *The psychologist's eat anything diet*. Toronto: Popular Library.

Pelchat, M. L., and Rozin, P. 1982. The special role of nausea in the acquisition of food dislikes by humans. *Appetite*, 3: 341–51.

Pelto, G. H. See Kandel, Jerome, and Pelto.

Peryam, D. R. 1963. The acceptance of novel foods. *Food Technology*, 17: 711–17.

Peryam, D. R. See also Kamen and Peryam.

Pierman, B. C., ed. 1978. *Color in the health care environment*. NBS special publication 516. Washington, D.C.: U.S. Department of Commerce.

Pierson, A., and LeMagnen, J. 1970. Study of food textures by recording of chewing and swallowing movements. *Journal of Texture Studies*, 1: 327–37.

Pilgrim, F. J. 1961. What foods do people accept or reject. *Journal of the American Dietetic Association*, 38: 439–43.

Pilgrim, F. J., and Kamen, J. M. 1959. Patterns of food preferences through factor analysis. *Marketing*, 24: 68.

Pilgrim, F. J. See also Siegel and Pilgrim.

Pliner, P. 1982. The effects of mere exposure on liking for edible substances. *Appetite*, 2: 283–90.

Pliner, P. See also Fallon, Rozin, and Pliner.

Prattala, R., and Keinonen, M. 1984. The use and the attributions of some sweet foods. *Appetite*, 5: 199–207.

Pryor, B. See Biggers and Pryor.

Rao, D. B. 1975. Problems of nutrition in the aged. *Journal of the American Geriatrics Society*, 22: 62–65.

Restaurants and Institutions 1985. Vol. 95(25): 98–106.

Richter, C. P. 1942. Total self-regulatory functions in animals and human beings. *The Harvey Lectures*, 38: 63–103.

Rierdan, J. See Baker, Rierdan, and Napner.

Riggs, L. A. See Kling and Riggs.

Ringsdove, W. M., Jr. See Cheraskin, Ringsdove, and Brecher.

Rock, I. 1975. *An introduction to perception*. New York: Macmillan.

Rodin, J. 1980. The externality theory today. In A. J. Stunkard, ed., *Obesity*. Philadelphia: Saunders.

Rolls, B. J.; Rolls, E. T.; Rowe, E. A.; and Sweeney, K. 1981. Sensory-specific satiety in man. *Physiology and Behavior*, 27: 137–42.

Rolls, B. J.; Rowe, E. A.; and Rolls, E. T. 1980. Appetite and obesity: Influences of sensory stimuli and external cues. In M. R. Turner, ed., *Nutrition and Lifestyles*. London: Life Science Publishers.

Rolls, B. J.; Rowe, E. A.; Rolls, E. T.; Kingston, B.; Megson, A.; and Gunary, R. 1981. Variety in a meal enhances food intake in man. *Physiology and Behavior*, 26: 215–21.

Rolls, E. T. See Rolls, Rolls, Rowe, and Sweeney; Rolls, Rowe, and Rolls; Rolls, Rowe, Rolls, Kingston, Megson, and Gunary.

Rosch, E. 1977. Human categorization. In N. Warren, ed., *Studies in cross-cultural psychology*, vol 1. New York: Academic Press.

Rosenberg, M. J., and Hovland, C. I. 1960. Cognitive, affective, and behavioral components of attitudes. In C. I. Hovland and M. J. Rosenberg, eds., *Attitude organization and change*. New Haven: Yale University Press.

Ross, S., and Harriman, A. E. 1949. A preliminary study of the Crocker-Henderson odor classification system. *American Journal of Psychology*, 62: 399–404.

Rotter, J. See Birch, Marlin, and Rotter.

Rowe, E. A. See Rolls, Rolls, Rowe, and Sweeney; Rolls, Rowe, and Rolls; Rolls, Rowe, Rolls, Kingston, Megson, and Gunary.

Rozin, P., and Fallon, A. 1980. The psychological categorization of foods and nonfoods: A preliminary taxonomy of food rejections. *Appetite*, 1: 193–201.

Rozin, P.; Fallon, A.; and Mandell, R. 1984. Family resemblance in attitudes to foods. *Developmental Psychology*, 20(2): 309–14.

Rozin, P. See also Fallon, Rozin, and Pliner; Pelchat and Rozin.

Ryan, M. S. 1966. *Clothing: A study in human behavior*. New York: Holt, Rinehart & Winston.

Sallis, R. E., and Buckalew, L. W. 1984. Relation of capsule color and perceived potency. *Perceptual and Motor Skills*, 58: 897–98.

Sapir, E. 1969. Fashion. In R. R. Evans, ed., *Readings in collective behavior*. Chicago: Rand McNally.

Schafer, R. B. 1979. The self-concept as a factor in diet selection and quality. *Journal of Nutrition Education*, 2(1): 37–39.

Schafer, R. B., and Keith, D. J. 1978. Influences on food decisions across the family life cycle. *Journal of the American Dietetic Association*, 78: 144–48.

Schaie, K. W. 1961. Scaling the association between colors and mood-tones. *American Journal of Psychology*, 74: 266–73.

Schiffman, S. S., and Erickson, R. P. 1971. A psychophysical model for gustatory quality. *Physiology and Behavior*, 7: 617–33.

Schlosberg, H. See Woodworth and Schlosberg.

Schlundt, D. G. See Dubbert, Johnson, Schlundt, and Montague.

Schutz, H. G. 1954. Color in relation to food preference. In *Color in foods: A symposium*. Chicago: Quartermaster Food and Container Institute.

Serban, G., ed. 1975. *Nutrition and mental functions*. New York: Plenum.

Sexton, D. E. 1974. Differences in food shopping habits by areas of residence, race and income. *Journal of Retailing*, 50: 37–48.

Sheerer, M. See Goldstein and Sheerer.

Sherif, C. W. See Sherif and Sherif.

Sherif, M. 1935. A study of some social factors in perception. *Archives of Psychology*, no. 187.

Sherif, M., and Sherif, C. W. 1956. *An outline of social psychology* (rev. ed). New York: Harper & Row.

Sherif, M., and Sherif, C. W. 1969. *Social psychology*. New York: Harper & Row.

Sherwood, J. J. See Wagner and Sherwood.

Sherwood, S. 1973. Sociology of food and eating: Implications for action for the elderly. *American Journal of Clinical Nutrition*, 26: 1108–10.

Shiffman, H. R. 1976. *Sensation and perception: An integrated approach*. New York: Wiley.

Siegel, D. S., and Pilgrim, F. J. 1958. The effect of monotony on the acceptance of food. *American Journal of Psychology*, 71: 756–59.

Sigel, I. E. 1954. The dominance of meaning. *Journal of Genetic Psychology*, 85: 201–7.

Simoons, F. J. 1983. Geography and genetics as factors in the psychobiology of human food selection. In L. M. Barker, ed., *The psychology of human food selection*. Westport, Conn.: AVI.

Sims, L. S. See Grotkowski and Sims.

Singer, J. E. See Baum, Singer, and Valins.

Singer, R. See Leventhal, Singer, and Jones.

Singer, R. D. See Blackman, Singer, and Mertz.

Smelser, N. L. 1963. *Theory of collective behavior.* New York: The Free Press of Glencoe.

Solberg, P. See Zubek and Solberg.

Sommer, R. 1969. *Personal space: The behavioral basis of design.* Englewood Cliffs, N.J.: Prentice-Hall.

Sommer, R. 1974. *Tight spaces: Hard architecture and how to humanize it.* Englewood Cliffs, N.J.: Prentice-Hall.

Statistical abstracts of the United States 1982 (December). Washington, D.C.: U.S. Department of Commerce, Bureau of the Census.

Steiner, J. E. 1977. Facial expressions of the neonate infant indicating the hedonics of food-related chemical stimuli. In J. M. Weiffenbach, ed., *Taste and development.* Bethesda, Md.: U.S. Department of Health, Education, and Welfare.

Stellar, E. 1954. The physiology of motivation. *Psychological Review,* 61: 5–22.

Stevens, S. S., and Davis, H. 1938. *Hearing.* New York: Wiley.

Stunkard, A. J. See Garb and Stunkard.

Sweeney, K. See Rolls, Rolls, Rowe, and Sweeney.

Szczesniak, A. S. 1963. Classification of textural characteristics. *Journal of Food Science,* 28: 385–89.

Szczesniak, A. S. 1966 (October). Texture measurements (symposium). *Food Technology,* 20: 52–58.

Szczesniak, A. S. 1971. Consumer awareness of texture and of other food attributes, II. *Journal of Texture Studies,* 2: 196–206.

Szczesniak, A. S. 1975. General Foods texture profile revisited—ten-year perspective. *Journal of Texture Studies,* 6: 5–17.

Szczesniak, A. S. 1979. Classification of mouthfeel characteristics of beverages. In P. Sherman, ed., *Food texture and rheology.* New York: Academic Press.

Szczesniak, A. S., and Kahn, E. L. 1971. Consumer awareness of and attitudes to food texture. *Journal of Texture Studies,* 2: 280–95.

Szczesniak, A. S.; Loew, B. J.; and Skinner, E. Z. 1975. Consumer texture profile technique. *Journal of Food Science,* 40: 1253–56.

Tempro, W. A. 1978. Nutritional problems in the aged: Dietary aspects. *Journal of the American Medical Association,* 70: 281–83.

Thompson, G. G. 1962. *Child psychology* (2nd ed.). Boston: Houghton Mifflin.

Thornton, J. See Kissileff, Gruss, Thornton, and Jordan.

Thurstone, L. L. 1946. Comment. *American Journal of Sociology,* 52: 39–40.

Todhunter, E. N. 1973. Food habits, food fadism, and nutrition. *World Review of Nutrition and Dietetics,* 16: 286.

Tuorila-Ollikainen, H., and Mahlamaki-Kultanen, S. 1985. The relationship of attitudes and experiences of Finnish youths to their hedonic responses to sweetness in soft drinks. *Appetite,* 6: 115–24.

Turner, R. H., and Killian, L. M. 1972. *Collective behavior* (2nd ed.). Englewood Cliffs, N.J.: Prentice-Hall.

Valins, S. See Baum, Singer, and Valins.

Vermeersch, J. A. See Yperman and Vermeersch.

Vietmeyer, N. 1985. Immigrants from the vegetable kingdom. *Smithsonian,* 16: 34–43.

Wagner, R. V., and Sherwood, J. J. 1969. *The study of attitude change.* Belmont, Calif.: Brooks/Cole.

Wakefield, L. See Bass, Wakefield, and Kolassa.

Walford, J. 1980. Historical development of food coloration. In J. Walford, ed., *Developments in food colours—1*. London: Applied Science Publishers.

Warm, J. S. See Dember and Warm.

Washbon, M. B. See Gifft, Washbon, and Harrison.

Waterman, D. See Meiselman and Waterman.

Waters, J. C. E. See Lyman and Waters.

Watson, G. 1972. *Nutrition and your mind*. New York: Bantam.

Watts, J. C. See Leventhal, Watts, and Pagano.

Wexner, L. B. 1954. The degree to which colors (hues) are associated with mood-tones. *Journal of Applied Psychology*, 38: 432–35.

Wilentz, J. S. 1968. *The senses of man*. New York: Crowell.

Williams, S. R. 1974. *Essentials of nutrition and diet therapy*. St. Louis: Mosby.

Witkin, H. A. 1959. The perception of the upright. *Scientific American*, 200: 50–56.

Witkin, H. A., and Asch, S. E. 1948. Studies in space orientation. IV: Further experiments on perception of the upright with displaced visual fields. *Journal of Experimental Psychology*, 38: 762–82.

Witkin, H. A., and Berry, J. W. 1975. Psychological differentiation in cross-cultural perspective. *Journal of Cross-cultural Psychology*, 6: 4–87.

Woodworth, R. S. 1938. *Experimental Psychology*. New York: Holt.

Woodworth, R. S., and Schlosberg, H. 1954. *Experimental psychology* (rev. ed.). New York: Holt.

Worchel, S. 1974. The effect of three types of arbitrary thwarting on the instigation to aggression. *Journal of Personality*, 42: 300–318.

Worchel, S., and Cooper, J. 1983. *Understanding social psychology*. Homewood, Ill.: Dorsey Press.

Wright, R. H. 1964. *The science of smell*. New York: Basic Books.

Wright, R. H. 1966. Why is an odour? *Nature*, 209: 551–54.

Wurtman, J. J. See Wurtman and Wurtman.

Wurtman, R. I., and Wurtman, J. J. 1984. Nutrients, neurotransmitter synthesis, and the control of food intake. In A. J. Stunkard and E. Stellar, eds., *Eating and its disorders*. New York: Raven Press.

Wyant, K. W., and Meiselman, H. L. 1984. Sex and race differences in food preferences of military personnel. *Journal of the American Dietetic Association*, 84(2): 169–75.

Yperman, A. M., and Vermeersch, J. A. 1979. Factors associated with children's food habits. *Journal of Nutrition Education*, 11: 72–76.

Yurkin, M. A. See Krondl, Lay, Yurkin, and Coleman.

Yurkstas, A. A. 1965. The masticatory act. *Journal of Prosthetic Dentistry*, 15: 248–60.

Zajonc, R. B. 1968. Attitudinal effects of mere exposure. *Journal of Personality and Social Psychology Monograph Supplement*, 9(2), part 2: 1–27.

Zeisel, J. 1981. *Inquiry by design*. Monterey, Calif.: Brooks/Cole.

Zimmerman, S. I. See Birch, Zimmerman, and Hind.

Zubek, J., and Solberg, P. 1954. *Human development*. New York: McGraw-Hill.

Zuckerman, M. 1979. *Sensation seeking: Beyond the optimal level of arousal*. Hillsdale, N.J.: Erlbaum.

INDEX